Longman Study Texts

She Stoops to Conquer

Longman Study Texts

General editor: Richard Adams

Titles in the series

Oliver Goldsmith

She Stoops to Conquer

edited by
Neil King

with a personal essay by
Irving Wardle

Longman

LONGMAN GROUP UK LIMITED
Longman House
Burnt Mill, Harlow, Essex CM20 2JE, England
and Associated Companies throughout the world.

First published 1985
Tenth impression 1993

Set in Linotron 202 Baskerville 10/12 point

Produced by Longman Singapore Publishers Pte Ltd
Printed in Singapore

ISBN   0-582-33167-6

The Publisher's policy is to use paper manufactured from
sustainable forests.

Contents

Contents

A personal essay

by Irving Wardle

Goldsmith's human toybox

As a theatre reviewer I see about two hundred plays a year, and as I have been doing the job for twenty years you don't need a calculator to work out my total score. It happens that during all those nights out, I have never seen a production of *She Stoops to Conquer*. I did, however, see it as a school play when I was about fifteen, and I remember that cast very well. Tony Lumpkin was terrific: a fact I resented at the time, as he was played by a 15-stone bully called Duggie who made my life a misery whenever we went on Dig for Victory camps (this was in the war). Young Marlow had real star casting in the person of the super-sophisticated head boy, Dennis, a gifted saxophone player who had lately scandalized the staff by turning up at a dance in the gym with a divorced lady on his arm; and who then departed for Oxford in a blaze of glory before settling down to his life's work with a firm that manufactured meat-pie-making machines.

When I opened my ancient copy of Goldsmith, I also found that I remembered the play very well: not only the main characters and story line, but whole stretches of dialogue that had stayed in my mind almost word for word. It was like going up to an attic and finding a dusty old box full of apples still as firm and sharp-flavoured as if they had just been picked.

Plays and books that have that effect are usually called classics, but I am trying to avoid that term. A 'classic' sounds like something you have to admire from a respectful distance. When I come across the word in textbooks I often have the feeling that I am being sold something unpalatable for my own good. Also, there are any number of genuine classics that turn out to be bruised and withered when you open the box.

She Stoops to Conquer belongs to a small group of English comedies that belong to everybody, like the English countryside. Others include Jonson's *The Alchemist*, Sheridan's *The School for Scandal*, and Wilde's *The Importance of Being Earnest*. There is no collective term for them. All you can say is that they go straight into your head and stay there like a good tune. They are never fashionable because they never go out of fashion; and they seem to have come into existence with a single, perfectly aimed stroke.

This is not true of other plays by the same men. With Jonson's 'humour' comedies, or Wilde's high-society pieces, you are very conscious of the author, stripped to the waist behind the scenes, labouring away to turn a comic theory into something funny, or contrive something to give the genteel audience some daring laughs and then send them home with a good old-fashioned moral to chew over. Nor is it true of Goldsmith, who hardly ranks as a professional playwright at all. His only other play, *The Good Natur'd Man*, had a ten-night run at Covent Garden in 1768 and then vanished for nearly two centuries: a fact that surprised nobody who saw the National Theatre revival in 1971. However, after this lame start he went on to produce *She Stoops to Conquer* and promptly achieved theatrical immortality; just as he won a permanent place among English poets with *The Deserted Village*, and took possession of the novel with *The Vicar of Wakefield*. It was his habit to do something perfectly and then move on to something else.

That is the unfairness of genius, and it is the kind of thing that drives capable, minor artists to despair: especially so in Goldsmith's time, when 'inspiration' was mistrusted and achievement was seen as the reward of diligent practice. Among his busy, hard-working contemporaries for whom 'nature's chief good is writing well', Goldsmith sits like a lone angler waiting for a prize fish to nibble the hook.

That image is not mine: I have stolen it from the French playwright Jean Anouilh. For Anouilh, there is no point in setting out to write a play. All you can do is wait for one to appear and then seize it. The best angler in the world will catch nothing if he throws his line into the Dead Sea; and the same applies to the writer. Either there is a play there or not.

That sounds too obvious to be worth saying, but I have had enough dire evenings in the theatre to believe that it can never be said too often. Bad plays need not be badly written. They may tackle important themes with great intelligence. They may have well-drawn characters and brilliantly funny lines. They may contain every part of the dramatic anatomy, and still come over as creaking, lopsided robots for want of the central idea that transforms a mechanical invention into a living organism. It would be sentimental to describe this vital component as a heart: some good plays are brutal to the point of heartlessness. You might compare it to a spoonful of yoghurt culture, capable of passing on its own life to any quantity of raw milk. I am not pushing that comparison. But after sitting through so many artificially constructed plays, often put together by highly intelligent and talented men, I know the rush of grateful recognition when the real thing comes along.

Here are some words of advice from J B Priestley, our greatest expert on dramatic construction. He is laying down the rules for different kinds of play.

Would you like a play in which the action tightly unwinds like a coiled spring and every single speech develops the situation, but a play too in which the characters are all created and exhibited in the round? Yes, you would. So would I. And it can't be done. Large characters in the round need plenty of space and therefore a certain looseness of construction, which immediately rules out any tight economical handling, any action uncoiling like a spring. Take your choice, but don't ask for both at once.

The Art of the Dramatist (Heinemann, 1957)

That makes good sense if you apply it to Priestley's own plays, and to a great many others as well. In *The Comedy of Errors* you will find Shakespeare confirming Priestley's argument.

Here is an extreme example of an action unwinding like a spring and throwing up a non-stop succession of comic disasters. Shakespeare achieves this effect through mathematical plotting, and reducing the characters (led by two sets of identical twins) to ciphers. One spontaneous human reaction and the machine would collapse in ruins.

Alternatively, take a play like John Osborne's *Look Back in Anger*, which was immensely exciting to my generation in the 1950s whatever you may think of it as an O level text. All the mute dissatisfaction and political disgust of the post-war young found a marvellous spokesman in the cantankerous figure of Osborne's Jimmy Porter. But as the rest of the play is there to trigger off Jimmy's tirades, there is no sign of a coiled spring; rather a toy car that only moves when pushed. You cannot say this is a fault in the play, because if Osborne had tightened the plot and allowed the defenceless surrounding characters to start answering back, he would only have cramped Jimmy's style. So once again Priestley seems to be right.

He is not right, though, when it comes to Goldsmith. The subtitle of *She Stoops to Conquer* is *The Mistakes of a Night*: almost the same as *The Comedy of Errors*. We are back in the coiled-spring department. Everything hinges on misunderstandings. Marlow mistakes the Hardcastles' house for an inn and their daughter for a servant. Mrs Hardcastle mistakes flattery for real admiration, and imagines her son to be in love with her niece. Marlow is variously mistaken for a hopeless weed and an arrogant lout. Mrs Hardcastle flops out of her carriage mistaking the bottom of her garden for Crack-skull Common and her husband for a highwayman. The intricate apparatus of the foiled elopement, the jewel theft, and the frustrated dash to Aunt Pedigree's depends on split-second timing; and, as in Shakespeare, one unguarded word and the whole thing would grind to a stop.

It is a most beautiful piece of mathematical plotting. But Goldsmith, being more than a constructor of plots, expresses his mathematics in flesh and blood. He sees no reason to make the choice between action and character. He does ask for both at once. And he achieves the miracle of a play combining in-humanly mechanical precision with the always unpredictable human element. It is rather like a chess match played with real kings, bishops and knights, who may take it into their heads to move anywhere on the board, but who still manage to enact a masterly game.

The Hardcastle parents, Tony and Kate, are as fully rounded as characters in a Victorian novel (more so, I would say, than in the work of a bullying character-manipulator like Dickens). They may not have the same room to expand, but is Anouilh's fish cramped because it happens not to be a Dickensian elephant? The essential point is that these people exist as vital parts in a living organism, as I think you will agree when you get to know the play.

Look closely at any of their scenes and you will find it im-possible to tell whether the characters are there to advance the plot, or the plot to illuminate the characters. The opening scene is as good an example as any. As in countless other opening scenes, two characters are swapping information so as to clue the audience in to the story: a highly artificial procedure known as the exposition. Some writers make it more credible by staging it as a meeting between strangers, or an interview in which only one of the speakers is in the know. Goldsmith makes things hard-er for himself by bringing on an old married couple who can only tell each other things they already know inside out. They know their house looks like an inn. They know Tony is throwing his money about on drink. It is no news to Mr Hardcastle to learn that his wife was formerly married to a Mr Lumpkin, and it is all Mrs Hardcastle can do to stop herself screaming when her husband starts in on his war stories.

The last detail suggests how Goldsmith gets himself out of trouble. He picks a situation in which people do tell each other what they know already: a family squabble. The Hardcastles have been bickering like this for years. He is never going to tease her out of her vanity or her dream of getting into smart society; she is never going to bully him out of his stick-in-the-mud affection for provincial obscurity and the good old times. But meanwhile they keep up the fight like two weary old pugs throwing the same punches over and over again; and, incidentally, telling us everything we need to know. What is information to us is ammunition to them.

There is more to the scene than that. Look at it in isolation and you can fairly describe the exposition as the by-product of a family squabble. Connect it with what follows and you see the whole comedy developing out of the opening skirmish. It is a comedy of divided viewpoints. Mr and Mrs Hardcastle have contradictory opinions about Tony. So do we. Is he a selfish, thick-witted oaf, or a good-natured chap with plenty of brains when he needs them? (Both true, as it turns out; just as both views of Marlow are false.) The Hardcastles are similarly divided on wider issues. Novelty versus tradition. Genteel versus country manners. Arranged marriages versus love matches. And lurking in the background is the grand Shakespearian debate on nature versus nurture.

First sounded in the opening conversation, these themes branch out and become the play. And just as neither of the Hardcastles is ever going to win the argument, so the play exercises its themes without allowing victory to either side. Even true love is squared with financial convenience. And the general harmony of the ending is achieved through a compromise that leaves the issues still wide open. It is the privilege of the artist simply to show life, and leave moral judgements to other people.

You may detect a flaw in this argument in the disagreeable person of Mrs Hardcastle. If Goldsmith is trying to strike an impartial balance between the two sides, why does he weight the scales so heavily against her? You will begin to see why if you read the section in Neil King's Introduction on 'Sentimental comedy': a form of entertainment which Dr Goldsmith diagnosed as a disease threatening the life of the English theatre. This is how he describes it:

In these plays almost all the characters are good, and exceedingly generous; they are lavish enough with their tin money on the stage; and though they want humour, have abundance of sentiment and feeling. If they happen to have faults or foibles, the spectator is taught, not only to pardon, but to applaud them in consideration of the goodness of their hearts; so that folly, instead of being ridiculed, is commended, and the comedy aims at touching our passions without the power of being truly pathetic.

'Sentimental Comedy', No. XXII

If you want a modern equivalent, think of a play featuring the perfect people – doting parents, happy children, lovable old gran – in a television commercial: a debased form asserting what the American writer Norman Mailer calls 'the tyranny of the totally pleasant personality'. Eighteenth-century audiences had fallen victim to an epidemic of this stuff, and we can be sure that if Mrs Hardcastle had managed to get her trip to London she would have lapped it up. To prove this, Goldsmith stages a sentimental comedy under her own roof. The smooth-tongued Hastings, and Marlow when he is on his best behaviour, are models of sentimental etiquette; and she accepts their well-bred compliments and fine feelings, never suspecting any duplicity. As a result she gets taken, literally, for a ride, and learns the difference between what people say and what they do.

In that sense, she is a caricature of the sentimentally addicted London playgoer. Look, Goldsmith is saying to the house, you have been duped long enough. You don't mistake tin money for the real thing: why let yourself be cheated with counterfeit emotions? You know what people are really like: look at yourselves. Do you want to be like Marlow, so twisted up with gentility and moral posturing that you can never be yourself except with people you despise?

That in itself, of course, is a moral lecture; and Goldsmith would himself be falling into the sentimental trap if he delivered it directly. Instead, he leaves you to work it out from the stage picture, which presents the traditional comic contrast between town and country. Go back to the Restoration dramatists at the turn of the eighteenth century and you find a world of elegant, witty Londoners having fun at the expense of clodhopping squires and rustic heiresses mad keen to get their hands on a London husband. 'All beyond Hyde Park's a desert' was the Restoration slogan. It was no slogan for Goldsmith, who had wandered around Europe playing his flute, and regarded himself as a citizen of the world. So he turns the Restoration formula inside out; and what you see is a society of lively, spontaneous country folk lumbered with a party of fashion-plate guests who are half-stifled with good-breeding. The mere sight of these two groups on stage should get the main message across. Look at Garrick's Prologue. 'Faces are blocks', he says, 'in sentimental scenes.' There speaks the frustrated actor who knows what it is to be stuck with a string of unplayable parts.

The same contrast appears in the plotting. Hastings attempts a conventional elopement and bites the dust, whereupon Tony takes over and gets him out of trouble. When orthodox romantic intrigue fails, rustic improvisation comes to the rescue. But the main contrast appears, most wonderfully, in the dialogue. At one extreme there is the language of Marlow's interview scene, caricaturing the limp fatuities of the sentimental style as he ties himself up in verbal knots. At the other is Tony's rich vernacular, bounding along with virile rhythms and piercing local imagery that jumps off the page, so that you hear his voice and see his beery frame lashing the horses through the mud, or bored out of his mind in the music room watching cousin Con's 'pretty long fingers, that she twists this way and that, over the haspicholls, like a parcel of bobbins.' Moving inwards from the extremes, you find Mr Hardcastle's manly, vigorously flavoured speech set against the colourless correctness of Hastings.

Dead centre is Kate, a girl whose natural idiom is the cool, candid English of Jane Austen; but who can leap the class and regional boundaries and speak the dialect of the sentimental salon or the alehouse as it suits her. She is the one free agent among a set of characters fettered by upbringing and social ties.

In that sense she is the winner, and *She Conks to Stupor* (as it was
known at my school) is her play. When you ask what she has
won, another perspective opens up. Obviously she gets her man,
but she also wins for other people in the story; and her specta-
tors have a chance of winning too, if they accept her invitation to
shed their blinkered prejudices, stop treating their fellow creatures as if they belonged to alien tribes; and learn to feel at home
in the world.

Introduction

Oliver Goldsmith (1728–74)

Born in Ireland of Anglo-Irish parents, Goldsmith inherited his benevolent and unworldly temperament from his father, a clergyman who may well have been Goldsmith's model when he came to write *The Vicar of Wakefield* (1766). His childhood was not altogether happy: it seems that fun was frequently made of his smallpox scarred face, his clumsiness, and his tendency to make blunders. At sixteen years of age he entered Trinity College, Dublin, as a sizar – that is, a poor scholar who, instead of paying fees, performed menial tasks such as waiting at table and sweeping floors. After an uneven career he just managed to gain a pass degree in 1749. He had already begun to write in order to help his financial state, some of his earliest poems being sold for five shillings each and sung as street ballads.

Rejected by the Church, the calling intended for him by his father, he turned his hand to many activities. First, he returned to his native village, where he wrote a little but spent much time in the public house, like his creation Tony Lumpkin. He began to study law in Dublin, but gambled away the £50 living allowance which his uncle had given him (he remained an unsuccessful gambler all his life). The patient uncle again lent him money, and in 1752 he went to Scotland to study medicine for two years. Again, he did not finish the course, but went off wandering across Europe 'with a guinea in his pocket, one shirt to his back, and a flute in his hand'. His flute-playing kept him in bread, and he also begged and borrowed; sometimes he 'sang for his supper' by disputing with European academics and intellectuals, accepting their hospitality in return for his entertaining and lively conversations (Goldsmith also had the reputation of frequently talking rubbish). In his travels he gained a wide experience which was valuable in his later writings. He claimed that he qualified abroad as a doctor, and thereafter called himself 'Doctor Goldsmith'. The occasions later on which he attempted to practise medicine were failures, and he probably contributed to his own death by insisting upon treating himself. A friend once advised him that he should only prescribe medicine for his enemies. It seems that in several respects Goldsmith was doomed to be fascinated by activities at which he was incompetent.

He arrived in England in 1756, and tried in turn to earn his living as a chemist's assistant, a proof reader for the printer and novelist Samuel Richardson, and a teacher, settling down in 1759 to the life of a writer. He churned out endless writings in return for little money, which he always spent with glee as soon as he received it, and usually upon his friends rather than himself. Most of his great mass of writing is of small interest today; however, his style and fluency brought him the praise and friendship of several notable men, including the great literary figure of Dr Samuel Johnson (1709–84) and the painter Sir Joshua Reynolds (1723–92). The measure of their esteem for Goldsmith is that they made him one of the nine founder members of their famous literary club.

By the early 1760s Goldsmith was making a fair living from his writing, but he was as carefree as ever with his money. On one occasion, Johnson received an urgent summons from his friend, who was about to be arrested by his landlady for debt. Johnson sent a guinea ahead of him; when he arrived, he found that Goldsmith had laid out his guinea on a bottle of Madeira. However, Johnson took away from that visit the manuscript of *The Vicar of Wakefield* and sold it to a publisher on Goldsmith's behalf. That book of gentle humour and delicate irony quickly became established as one of the best loved of English novels. Johnson had previously encouraged him to complete *The Traveller* (1764), a poem which owed much to his travels, and which had led many to recognize his ability with the pen. His literary reputation was confirmed by his poem *The Deserted Village* (1770), in which he laments the economic policies which were causing a depopulation of the countryside.

His first play, *The Good Natur'd Man* (1768) was not a success. The over-refined taste of the time considered certain aspects of the play to be 'low'. His second play, *She Stoops to Conquer*, was surrounded by problems before it reached the stage. During the first performance, a miserable Goldsmith was found by a friend wandering around St James's Park, and was persuaded that he should be at the theatre in case he was needed. He entered at the stage door in time to hear a great hiss rise from the audience (see note [page 105] to *She thinks ... miles off*). Colman, the theatre manager, snapped at him: 'We have been sitting these three hours on a barrel of gunpowder.' No doubt he was annoyed that he had been proved wrong (see note [page 81] on *your partiality* ...), for the play was a great success. Instead of the expected hostility, Goldsmith's friends in the audience found themselves surrounded by enthusiastic theatregoers.

He continued to write all kinds of less prominent material, and it seems probable that overwork, allied with the worry of enormous debts caused by his continual overspending, led to his decline and death at a comparatively early age.

Throughout his life his pockmarked face, clumsy ways and unpredictable conversation led many to see him as a mere buffoon. Johnson saw the truth when he said, 'No man was more foolish when he had not a pen in his hand, nor more wise when he had'. Horace Walpole described him as an inspired idiot. He was also cheerful, kind-hearted, spendthrift, and generous to a fault. His writing is among the clearest and most readable in the English language, and he deserves the memorial which his friends placed in Westminster Abbey.

Sentimental comedy

Audiences find *She Stoops to Conquer* as funny today as they did two hundred years ago; and the play has an added relish if we understand that Goldsmith was presenting the case against 'refined' sentimental comedies which were very popular at the time amongst the London theatregoing public. Goldsmith complained that, since the exhilarating, if vulgar, Restoration style of comedy had gone out of fashion, stage comedies were no longer funny.

During the eigtheenth century, audiences had become more middle class, and they had little time for the extravagant behaviour and devil-may-care wit of aristocratic Restoration comedy. What they wanted was a straightforward, no-nonsense story, preferably one which abounded in moral sayings and worldly-wise sentiments. The plot should endorse the middle-class values of hard work and thrift. Comedy of manners was replaced by sentimental comedy such as Sir Richard Steele's *The Conscious Lovers* (1722) or Hugh Kelly's *False Delicacy* (1768). In these plays, virtue triumphed after difficulties and setbacks, and the audience was expected to show its emotional relief by weeping openly. *The Conscious Lovers* includes rather trivial love scenes, an attack upon duelling (nasty upper-class practice), and a long speech on the virtue of industriousness.

In *She Stoops*, sentimental comedy is gently mocked on account of: (1) its love of 'sentiments' – that is, superficial and pompous moral statements (see Garrick's Prologue); (2) its lack of naturalism (again, see the Prologue); (3) its genteel dislike of 'low' characters (see Act I, scene 2, after the song: Goldsmith is taunting those who hissed at the 'low' scene in *The Good Natur'd Man*). In Goldsmith's *Essay on the Theatre; or, a Comparison between Laughing and Sentimental Comedy*, he also condemns that latter's dull dialogue, its episodes of pathos in which the audience is invited to weep rather than laugh, and its use of 'good', refined characters who are usually taken from high society, and are often titled.

In view of the popularity of sentimental comedy, it can be understood why Colman, the manager of the Covent Garden Theatre (see page xviii above and the note on the Dedication, page 81), was so worried about producing the play and felt during the first night that he was sitting upon a keg of gunpowder. Goldsmith would have been satisfied if he had known that future audiences all round the world would still be laughing at his 'Laughing Comedy', when eighteenth-century sentimental comedies would be hidden in obscure corners of university libraries, their titles unremembered.

She Stoops to Conquer

Goldsmith's 'mistake of a night'

Many writers base their stories on events which have actually happened to them. The main impetus of the plot of *She Stoops* comes from a boyhood experience when Oliver asked his way to the nearest inn. He did not realize that he had enquired of the local practical joker, who promptly directed him to the home of a wealthy gentleman, Squire Featherstone:

> Oliver rang at the gate ... and was shown as a supposed guest into the parlour of the Squire ... Mr Featherstone, unlike the excellent but explosive Mr Hardcastle, is said to have seen the mistake and humoured it. Oliver had a supper which gave him so much satisfaction, that he ordered a bottle of wine to follow; and the attentive landlord was not only forced to drink with him, but, with like familiar condescension, the wife and pretty daughter were invited to the supper room. Going to bed [Oliver] stopped to give special instructions for a hot cake to breakfast, and it was not till be had dispatched this meal, and was looking at his guinea with pathetic aspect of farewell, that the truth was told him by the good-natured Squire.
>
> from John Forster's biography of Goldsmith,
> published in 1848.

The comedy

It is always difficult to assess what makes something funny, for n exploring the comedy we tend to destroy the joke. However, certain basic devices can be detected by which Goldsmith makes us laugh.

In *She Stoops*, much of the audience's mirth is derived from dramatic irony. What does this mean? 'Irony' is a term used to described words which are charged with a layer of meaning different from the literal one, the subtler interpretation of which the speaker or hearer is sometimes unaware. More specifically, 'dramatic irony' is a term used to describe a situation in which the speaker is unaware of the significance of what he is saying, but the audience and perhaps some of the other characters are 'in the know'.

The principal source of dramatic irony in the play is, of course, Marlow's delusion that he is staying in an inn. Goldsmith carefully prepares the ground in Act I, scene 1, where Hardcastle and his house are depicted as old-fashioned and provincial. Mrs Hardcastle has pretensions to refinement, but her behaviour merely emphasizes her naivety. Hence, when Marlow and Hastings arrive in Act II, we can quite believe that the house could be mistaken for an inn. As the play proceeds and other characters find out about the mistake, they join us in the joke, so helping to heighten the irony as Marlow is increasingly isolated in his blissful ignorance of the truth. Other examples of dramatic irony abound in the play: the affair of Constance's jewels; Kate's pretence of being the barmaid and the consequent manifestation of Marlow's 'other' character; the 'wild goose chase' in Act V ... One could go on to explore and analyse this in detail, and *you* should do so.

All the funny mistakes which occur in the play, and the complicated situations which arise and from which the characters then attempt to extricate themselves, have led some to say that *She Stoops* is little more than a farce (that is, drama which merely stimulates laughter and has little depth in characterization or theme). In a review on 16 March 1773 the *Morning Chronicle* reported that 'the audience are kept in a continual roar', and the *London Magazine* considered that 'consistency is repeatedly violated for the sake of humour ... in lieu of comedy he [Goldsmith] has sometimes presented us with farce'. The implication of calling the play a farce is that it is merely a caricature of real life, and that it has no realistic depth. It is true that there are elements of caricature: for instance, Mr Hardcastle and Tony Lumpkin are, in their likes and habits, eighteenth-century Londoners' stock images of two kinds of country squire. However, when examined closely, Mr Hardcastle emerges as the most complex character in the play – foolish, knowing, grumbling, kindly, opinionated, forgiving and, despite these paradoxical qualities, believable; and Tony is a great deal more than the 'brainless practical joker' which one critic has called him. For much of the play he is the clever manipulator of the action. Mrs Hardcastle is a fine comic character. She is the foolish, doting mother who is desperate to be abreast of the fashion and 'up with the Joneses'; and she is not to be seen, as she sometimes has been, as merely the only unsympathetic character in the play. Otherwise, how do we explain her instinctive readiness in Act V to give her life for her son? Goldsmith's genius is that he can give us characters who are both funny and serious; and that he can create a variety of situations which quickly develop side by side, all of them coming together and resolving themselves at the end.

Goldsmith's own term, 'a Laughing Comedy', must not be forgotten. He wrote the play to amuse, and was not trying for psychological depth or profound social comment; yet there emerges a natural, unforced richness.

Hero and heroine

Marlow is a strange kind of hero, in that most of the dramatic irony is at his expense. He is made a fool of by Tony, and by Kate when she 'stoops to conquer' him, and is laughed at – albeit good-naturedly – by nearly everbody when the truth is revealed. He is acutely sensitive to ridicule which he may suffer at the hands of the smart town set:

... I shall be laugh'd at over the whole town, I shall be stuck up in caricatura in all the print shops.

Act IV (page 54)

Also, Goldsmith has him displaying the 'sentiments' so beloved of the town audiences. At one point he says to Kate:

I can never harbour a thought of seducing simplicity that trusted in my honour, or bringing ruin upon one, whose only fault was being too lovely.... I owe too much to the opinion of the world, too much to the authority of a father, so that – I can scarcely speak it – it affects me.

Act IV (page 55)

and this is in a play which is noted for its natural conversation, clear language and short speeches.

Yet one point of the play is that a country girl conquers Marlow's affections – and his affectations; by implication, she triumphs over the values of the town which she perceives clearly. When reporting Marlow's advances to her, she says that he

Said some civil things of my face, talked much of his want of merit, and the greatness of mine; mentioned his heart, gave a short tragedy speech, and ended with pretended rapture.

Act V, scene 1

She deserves her conquest, for she has wit, resourcefulness and vitality in the tradition of Shakespeare's Rosalind in *As You Like It*. She is in control of the mistakes of the night, and knows what she wants to get out of them. Gently mocking, her influence is essentially beneficial and healing. She willingly allows herself to be thought of lowly class in order to allow Marlow's false city manner to drop, so that a genuine dialogue may develop between lovers. Her triumph is that, by 'getting her man', she unites town and country in marriage.

Incidentally, Constance too is sensible and determined. At

the opening of the play she has already decided whom she wishes to marry, and whereas Kate 'stoops to conquer', Constance must pretend that she loves Tony and thus 'stoop to dissimulation to avoid oppression'. Her attitude is not entirely romantic, but her name emphasizes the quality which brings her both love and fortune in the end.

Much additional background information on Goldsmith, *She Stoops to Conquer*, and on the eighteenth century in general can be found in the Notes to the text, which are located on pages 81–107.

She Stoops to Conquer

DEDICATION

TO SAMUEL JOHNSON, LL.D.

DEAR SIR,

By inscribing this slight performance to you, I do not mean so much to compliment you as myself. It may do me some honour to inform the public, that I have lived many years in intimacy with you. It may serve the interests of mankind also to inform them, that the greatest wit may be found in a character, without impairing the most unaffected piety.

I have, particularly, reason to thank you for your partiality to this performance. The undertaking a Comedy, not merely sentimental, was very dangerous; and Mr. Colman, who saw this piece in its various stages, always thought it so. However, I ventured to trust it to the public; and though it was necessarily delayed till late in the season, I have every reason to be grateful. I am,

Dear Sir,
Your most sincere
Friend and admirer,
OLIVER GOLDSMITH

PROLOGUE

BY DAVID GARRICK, ESQ

Enter MR. WOODWARD, *dressed in black, and holding a
Handkerchief to his Eyes*

*Excuse me, Sirs, I pray—I can't yet speak—
I'm crying now—and have been all the week!
'Tis not alone this mourning suit, good masters;
I've that within—for which there are no plasters!
Pray, would you know the reason why I'm crying?
The Comic muse, long sick, is now a-dying!
And if she goes, my tears will never stop;
For as a play'r, I can't squeeze out one drop;
I am undone, that's all—shall lose my bread—
I'd rather, but that's nothing—lose my head.
When the sweet maid is laid upon the bier,
Shuter and I shall be chief mourners here.
To her a mawkish drab of spurious breed,
Who deals in sentimentals, will succeed!
Poor Ned and I are dead to all intents;
We can as soon speak Greek as sentiments!
Both nervous grown, to keep our spirits up,
We now and then take down a hearty cup.
What shall we do?—if Comedy forsake us!
They'll turn us out, and no one else will take us.
But why can't I be moral?—Let me try—
My heart thus pressing—fix'd my face and eye—
With a sententious look, that nothing means,
(Faces are blocks in sentimental scenes)
Thus I begin—All is not gold that glitters,
Pleasure seems sweet, but proves a glass of bitters.
When ign'rance enters, folly is at hand:*

Learning is better far than house and land.
Let not your virtue trip, who trips may stumble,
And virtue is not virtue, if she tumble.

   I give it up—morals won't do for me;
To make you laugh I must play tragedy.
One hope remains—hearing the maid was ill,
A doctor comes this night to shew his skill.
To cheer her heart, and give your muscles motion,
He in five draughts prepar'd, presents a potion:
A kind of magic charm—for be assur'd,
If you will swallow it, the maid is cur'd:
But desperate the doctor, and her case is,
If you reject the dose, and make wry faces!
This truth he boasts, will boast it while he lives.
No pois'nous drugs are mix'd in what he gives;
Should he succeed, you'll give him his degree;
If not, within he will receive no fee!
The college you, must his pretensions back,
Pronounce him regular, or dub him quack.

CHARACTERS

in the play

MEN

SIR CHARLES MARLOW, *Mr. Gardner.*
YOUNG MARLOW (HIS SON), *Mr. Lewes.*
HARDCASTLE, *Mr. Shuter.*
HASTINGS, *Mr. Dubellamy.*
TONY LUMPKIN, *Mr. Quick.*
DIGGORY, *Mr. Saunders.*

WOMEN

MRS. HARDCASTLE, *Mrs. Green.*
MISS HARDCASTLE (KATE), *Mrs. Bulkley.*
MISS NEVILLE (CONSTANCE), *Mrs. Kniveton.*
MAID, *Miss Willems.*

LANDLORD, SERVANTS, &C., &C.

SHE STOOPS TO CONQUER

OR

THE MISTAKES OF A NIGHT

ACT I

SCENE, A CHAMBER IN AN OLD-FASHIONED
HOUSE

Enter MRS. HARDCASTLE *and* MR. HARDCASTLE

MRS. HARD: I vow, Mr. Hardcastle, you're very particular. Is there a creature in the whole country but ourselves, that does not take a trip to town now and then, to rub off the rust a little? There's the two Miss Hoggs, and our neighbour, Mrs. Grigsby, go to take a month's polishing every winter.

HARD: Ay, and bring back vanity and affectation to last them the whole year. I wonder why London cannot keep its own fools at home! In my time, the follies of the town crept slowly among us, but now they travel faster than a stage-coach. Its fopperies come down, not only as inside passengers, but in the very basket.

MRS. HARD: Ay, *your* times were fine times indeed; you have been telling us of *them* for many a long year. Here we live in an old rumbling mansion, that looks for all the world like an inn, but that we never see company. Our best visitors are old Mrs. Oddfish, the curate's wife, and little Cripplegate, the lame dancing-master: And all our entertainment your old stories of Prince Eugene and the Duke of Marlborough. I hate such old-fashioned trumpery.

HARD: And I love it. I love every thing that's old: old friends, old times, old manners, old books, old wines; and, I believe, Dorothy, (*taking her hand*) you'll own I have been pretty fond of an old wife.

MRS. HARD: Lord, Mr. Hardcastle, you're for ever at your Dorothy's, and your old wife's. You may be a Darby, but I'll be no Joan, I promise you. I'm not so old as you'd make me, by more than one good year. Add twenty to twenty, and make money of that.

HARD: Let me see; twenty added to twenty, makes just fifty and seven.

MRS. HARD: It's false, Mr. Hardcastle: I was but twenty when I was brought to bed of Tony, that I had by Mr. Lumpkin, my first husband; and he's not come to years of discretion yet.

HARD: Nor ever will, I dare answer for him. Ay, you have taught him finely.

MRS. HARD: No matter, Tony Lumpkin has a good fortune. My son is not to live by his learning. I don't think a boy wants much learning to spend fifteen hundred a year.

HARD: Learning, quotha! a mere composition of tricks and mischief.

MRS. HARD: Humour, my dear: nothing but humour. Come, Mr. Hardcastle, you must allow the boy a little humour.

HARD: I'd sooner allow him an horse-pond. If burning the footmen's shoes, frighting the maids, and worrying the kittens, be humour, he has it. It was but yesterday he fastened my wig to the back of my chair, and when I went to make a bow, I popt my bald head in Mrs. Frizzle's face.

MRS. HARD: And am I to blame? The poor boy was always too sickly to do any good. A school would be his death. When he comes to be a little stronger, who knows what a year or two's Latin may do for him?

HARD: Latin for him! A cat and fiddle. No, no, the ale-

house and the stable are the only schools he'll ever go
to.

MRS. HARD: Well, we must not snub the poor boy now, for
I believe we shan't have him long among us. Any body
that looks in his face may see he's consumptive.

HARD: Ay, if growing too fat be one of the symptoms.

MRS. HARD: He coughs sometimes.

HARD: Yes, when his liquor goes the wrong way.

MRS. HARD: I'm actually afraid of his lungs.

HARD: And truly so am I; for he sometimes whoops like a
speaking trumpet—(*Tony hallooing behind the Scenes*)—
O there he goes—a very consumptive figure, truly.

Enter TONY, *crossing the Stage*

MRS. HARD: Tony, where are you going, my charmer?
Won't you give Papa and I a little of your company,
lovee?

TONY: I'm in haste, Mother, I cannot stay.

MRS. HARD: You shan't venture out this raw evening, my
dear: You look most shockingly.

TONY: I can't stay, I tell you. The Three Pigeons expects
me down every moment. There's some fun going forward.

HARD: Ay; the ale-house, the old place; I thought so.

MRS. HARD: A low, paltry set of fellows.

TONY: Not so low neither. There's Dick Muggins the
exciseman, Jack Slang the horse doctor, little Aminadab
that grinds the music box, and Tom Twist that spins the
pewter platter.

MRS. HARD: Pray, my dear, disappoint them for one night
at least.

TONY: As for disappointing *them*, I should not so much
mind; but I can't abide to disappoint *myself*.

MRS. HARD (*Detaining him*): You shan't go.

TONY: I will, I tell you.

MRS. HARD: I say you shan't.

3

TONY: We'll see which is strongest, you or I.

[*Exit hauling her out*

HARD (*Solus*): Ay, there goes a pair that only spoil each other. But is not the whole age in a combination to drive sense and discretion out of doors? There's my pretty darling Kate; the fashions of the times have almost infected her too. By living a year or two in town, she is as fond of gauze, and French frippery, as the best of them.

Enter MISS HARDCASTLE

HARD: Blessings on my pretty innocence! Drest out as usual, my Kate. Goodness! What a quantity of superfluous silk has thou got about thee, girl! I could never teach the fools of this age, that the indigent world could be clothed out of the trimmings of the vain.

MISS HARD: You know our agreement, Sir. You allow me the morning to receive and pay visits, and to dress in my own manner; and in the evening, I put on my housewife's dress to please you.

HARD: Well, remember I insist on the terms of our agreement; and, by the by, I believe I shall have occasion to try your obedience this very evening.

MISS HARD: I protest, Sir, I don't comprehend your meaning.

HARD: Then to be plain with you, Kate, I expect the young gentleman I have chosen to be your husband from town this very day. I have his father's letter, in which he informs me his son is set out, and that he intends to follow himself shortly after.

MISS HARD: Indeed! I wish I had known something of this before. Bless me, how shall I behave? It's a thousand to one I shan't like him; our meeting will be so formal, and so like a thing of business, that I shall find no room for friendship or esteem.

HARD: Depend upon it, child, I'll never control your choice; but Mr. Marlow, whom I have pitched upon, is the son of my old friend, Sir Charles Marlow, of whom you have heard me talk so often. The young gentleman has been bred a scholar, and is designed for an employment in the service of his country. I am told he's a man of an excellent understanding.

MISS HARD: Is he?

HARD: Very generous.

MISS HARD: I believe I shall like him.

HARD: Young and brave.

MISS HARD: I'm sure I shall like him.

HARD: And very handsome.

MISS HARD: My dear Papa, say no more (*kissing his hand*), he's mine, I'll have him.

HARD: And to crown all, Kate, he's one of the most bashful and reserved young fellows in all the world.

MISS HARD: Eh! you have frozen me to death again. That word reserved, has undone all the rest of his accomplishments. A reserved lover, it is said, always makes a suspicious husband.

HARD: On the contrary, modesty seldom resides in a breast that is not enriched with nobler virtues. It was the very feature in his character that first struck me.

MISS HARD: He must have more striking features to catch me, I promise you. However, if he be so young, so handsome, and so every thing, as you mention, I believe he'll do still. I think I'll have him.

HARD: Ay, Kate, but there is still an obstacle. It's more than an even wager, he may not have *you*.

MISS HARD: My dear Papa, why will you mortify one so?—Well, if he refuses, instead of breaking my heart at his indifference, I'll only break my glass for its flattery. Set my cap to some newer fashion, and look out for some less difficult admirer.

HARD: Bravely resolved! In the mean time I'll go prepare

the servants for his reception; as we seldom see company
they want as much training as a company of recruits.
the first day's muster.   [Exit

MISS HARD (*Alone*): Lud, this news of Papa's, puts me
all in a flutter. Young, handsome; these he put last; but
I put them foremost. Sensible, good-natured; I like all
that. But then reserved, and sheepish, that's much against
him. Yet can't he be cured of his timidity, by being
taught to be proud of his wife? Yes, and can't I—But
I vow I'm disposing of the husband, before I have secured
the lover.

Enter MISS NEVILLE

MISS HARD: I'm glad you're come, Neville, my dear. Tell
me, Constance, how do I look this evening? Is there
any thing whimsical about me? Is it one of my well
looking days, child? Am I in face to-day?

MISS NEV: Perfectly, my dear. Yet now I look again—
bless me!—sure no accident has happened among the
canary birds or the gold fishes. Has your brother or the
cat been meddling? or has the last novel been too
moving?

MISS HARD: No; nothing of all this. I have been threatened
—I can scarcely get it out—I have been threatened with
a lover!

MISS NEV: And his name—

MISS HARD: Is Marlow.

MISS NEV: Indeed!

MISS HARD: The son of Sir Charles Marlow.

MISS NEV: As I live, the most intimate friend of Mr.
Hastings, *my* admirer. They are never asunder. I
believe you must have seen him when we lived in
town.

MISS HARD: Never.

MISS NEV: He's a very singular character, I assure you.
Among women of reputation and virtue, he is the

modestest man alive; but his acquaintances give him a very different character among creatures of another stamp: you understand me.

MISS HARD: An odd character, indeed. I shall never be able to manage him. What shall I do? Pshaw, think no more of him, but trust to occurrences for success. But how goes on your own affair my dear, has my mother been courting you for my brother Tony, as usual?

MISS NEV: I have just come from one of our agreeable tête-à-têtes. She has been saying a hundred tender things, and setting off her pretty monster as the very pink of perfection.

MISS HARD: And her partiality is such, that she actually thinks him so. A fortune like yours is no small temptation. Besides, as she has the sole management of it, I'm not surprised to see her unwilling to let it go out of the family.

MISS NEV: A fortune like mine, which chiefly consists in jewels, is no such mighty temptation. But at any rate if my dear Hastings be but constant, I make no doubt to be too hard for her at last. However, I let her suppose that I am in love with her son, and she never once dreams that my affections are fixed upon another.

MISS HARD: My good brother holds out stoutly. I could almost love him for hating you so.

MISS NEV: It is a good-natured creature at bottom, and I'm sure would wish to see me married to any body but himself. But my aunt's bell rings for our afternoon's walk round the improvements. Allons. Courage is necessary, as our affairs are critical.

MISS HARD: Would it were bed-time and all were well.

[*Exeunt*

SCENE, AN ALEHOUSE ROOM

Several shabby fellows with punch and tobacco. TONY *at the head of the table, a little higher than the rest: a mallet in his hand.*

OMNES: Hurrea, hurrea, hurrea, bravo.

FIRST FEL: Now, gentlemen, silence for a song. The Squire is going to knock himself down for a song.

OMNES: Ay, a song, a song!

TONY: Then I'll sing you, gentlemen, a song I made upon this alehouse, the Three Pigeons.

SONG

Let school-masters puzzle their brain,
  With grammar, and nonsense, and learning;
Good liquor, I stoutly maintain,
  Gives genus a better discerning.
Let them brag of their heathenish Gods,
  Their Lethes, their Styxes, and Stygians;
Their Quis, and their Quaes, and their Quods,
  They're all but a parcel of Pigeons.

  Toroddle, toroddle, toroll.

When Methodist preachers come down,
  A-preaching that drinking is sinful,
I'll wager the rascals a crown,
  They always preach best with a skinful.
For when you come down with your pence,
  For a slice of their scurvy religion,
I'll leave it to all men of sense,
  But you my good friend are the Pigeon.

  Toroddle, toroddle, toroll.

Then come, put the jorum about,
  And let us be merry and clever,

Our hearts and our liquors are stout,
  Here's the Three Jolly Pigeons for ever.
Let some cry up woodcock or hare,
  Your bustards, your ducks, and your widgeons;
But of all the gay birds in the air,
  Here's a health to the Three Jolly Pigeons.

                                    Toroddle, toroddle, toroll.

OMNES: Bravo, bravo.

FIRST FEL: The Squire has got spunk in him.

SECOND FEL: I loves to hear him sing, bekeays he never gives us nothing that's low.

THIRD FEL: O damn any thing that's low, I cannot bear it.

FOURTH FEL: The genteel thing is the genteel thing at any time. If so be that a gentleman bees in a concatenation accordingly.

THIRD FEL: I like the maxum of it, Master Muggins. What, though I am obligated to dance a bear, a man may be a gentleman for all that. May this be my poison, if my bear ever dances but to the very genteelest of tunes; Water Parted, or the minuet in Ariadne.

SECOND FEL: What a pity it is the Squire is not come to his own. It would be well for all the publicans within ten miles round of him.

TONY: Ecod and so it would Master Slang. I'd then shew what it was to keep choice of company.

SECOND FEL: O he takes after his own father for that. To be sure old Squire Lumpkin was the finest gentleman I ever set my eyes on. For winding the straight horn, or beating the thicket for a hare, or a wench, he never had his fellow. It was a saying in the place, that he kept the best horses, dogs and girls in the whole county.

TONY: Ecod, and when I'm of age, I'll be no bastard I promise you. I have been thinking of Bett Bouncer and the miller's grey mare to begin with. But come, my boys, drink about and be merry, for you pay no reckoning. Well Stingo, what's the matter?

Enter LANDLORD

LAND: There be two gentlemen in a post-chaise at the door. They have lost their way upo' the forest; and they are talking something about Mr. Hardcastle.

TONY: As sure as can be one of them must be the gentleman that's coming down to court my sister. Do they seem to be Londoners?

LAND: I believe they may. They look woundily like Frenchmen.

TONY: Then desire them to step this way, and I'll set them right in a twinkling. (*Exit* LANDLORD.) Gentlemen, as they mayn't be good enough company for you, step down for a moment, and I'll be with you in the squeezing of a lemon.   [*Exeunt mob*

TONY (*Solus*) Father-in-law has been calling me whelp, and hound, this half-year. Now if I pleased, I could be so revenged on the old grumbletonian. But then I'm afraid —afraid of what! I shall soon be worth fifteen hundred a year, and let him frighten me out of *that* if he can.

Enter LANDLORD, *conducting* MARLOW *and* HASTINGS

MARL: What a tedious uncomfortable day we have had of it! We were told it was but forty miles across the country, and we have come above threescore.

HAST: And all, Marlow, from that unaccountable reserve of yours, that would not let us inquire more frequently on the way.

MARL: I own, Hastings, I am unwilling to lay myself under an obligation to every one I meet: and often, stand the chance of an unmannerly answer.

HAST: At present, however, we are not likely to receive any answer.

TONY: No offence, gentlemen. But I'm told you have been inquiring for one Mr. Hardcastle in those parts. Do you know what part of the country you are in?

HAST: Not in the least, Sir, but should thank you for information.

TONY: Nor the way you came?

HAST: No, Sir; but if you can inform us——

TONY: Why, gentlemen, if you know neither the road you are going, nor where you are, nor the road you came, the first thing I have to inform you is, that—you have lost your way.

MARL: We wanted no ghost to tell us that.

TONY: Pray, gentlemen, may I be so bold as to ask the place from whence you came.

MARL: That's not necessary towards directing us where we are to go.

TONY: No offence; but question for question is all fair, you know. Pray, gentlemen, is not this same Hardcastle a cross-grain'd, old-fashion'd, whimsical fellow, with an ugly face; a daughter, and a pretty son?

HAST: We have not seen the gentleman, but he has the family you mention.

TONY: The daughter, a tall, trapesing, trolloping, talkative maypole—the son, a pretty, well-bred, agreeable youth, that every body is fond of.

MARL: Our information differs in this. The daughter is said to be well-bred and beautiful; the son, an aukward booby, reared up, and spoiled at his mother's apron-string.

TONY: He-he-hem!—Then, gentlemen, all I have to tell you is, that you won't reach Mr. Hardcastle's house this night, I believe.

HAST: Unfortunate!

TONY: It's a damn'd long, dark, boggy, dirty, dangerous way. Stingo, tell the gentlemen the way to Mr. Hardcastle's; (Winking upon the LANDLORD) Mr. Hardcastle's, of Quagmire Marsh, you understand me.

LAND: Master Hardcastle's! Lock-a-daisy, my masters, you're come a deadly deal wrong! When you came to

the bottom of the hill, you should have cross'd down
Squash-lane.

MARL: Cross down Squash-lane!

LAND: Then you were to keep straight forward, 'till you
came to four roads.

MARL: Come to where four roads meet!

TONY: Ay; but you must be sure to take only one of
them.

MARL: O Sir, you're facetious.

TONY: Then keeping to the right, you are to go sideways
'till you come upon Crack-skull Common: there you
must look sharp for the track of the wheel, and go forward,
'till you come to farmer Murrain's barn. Coming to the
farmer's barn, you are to turn to the right, and then to
the left, and then to the right about again, till you find
out the old mill——

MARL: Zounds, man! We could as soon find out the
longitude!

HAST: What's to be done, Marlow?

MARL: This house promises but a poor reception; though
perhaps the Landlord can accommodate us.

LAND: Alack, master, we have but one spare bed in the
whole house.

TONY: And to my knowledge, that's taken up by three
lodgers already. (*After a pause, in which the rest seem
disconcerted*) I have it. Don't you think, Stingo, our
landlady could accommodate the gentlemen by the fire-
side, with—three chairs and a bolster?

HAST: I hate sleeping by the fire-side.

MARL: And I detest your three chairs and a bolster.

TONY: You do, do you?—then let me see—what—if you
go on a mile further, to the Buck's Head; the old Buck's
Head on the hill, one of the best inns in the whole
county?

HAST: O ho! so we have escaped an adventure for this
night, however.

LAND (*Apart to* TONY): Sure, you ben't sending them to your father's as an inn, be you?

TONY: Mum, you fool you. Let *them* find that out. (*To them*) You have only to keep on straight forward, till you come to a large old house by the road side. You'll see a pair of large horns over the door. That's the sign. Drive up the yard and call stoutly about you.

HAST: Sir, we are obliged to you. The servants can't miss the way?

TONY: No, no: but I tell you though, the landlord is rich, and going to leave off business; so he wants to be thought a Gentleman, saving your presence, he! he! he! He'll be for giving you his company, and ecod if you mind him, he'll persuade you that his mother was an alderman, and his aunt a justice of peace.

LAND: A troublesome old blade to be sure; but a' keeps as good wines and beds as any in the whole country.

MARL: Well, if he supplies us with these, we shall want no further connexion. We are to turn to the right, did you say?

TONY: No, no; straight forward. I'll just step myself, and shew you a piece of the way. (*To the* LANDLORD) Mum.

LAND: Ah, bless your heart, for a sweet, pleasant—damn'd mischievous son of a whore.   [*Exeunt*

ACT II

SCENE, AN OLD-FASHIONED HOUSE

Enter HARDCASTLE, *followed by three or four aukward Servants*

HARD: Well, I hope you are perfect in the table exercise I have been teaching you these three days. You all know your posts and your places, and can shew that you have been used to good company, without ever stirring from home.

OMNES: Ay, ay.

HARD: When company comes, you are not to pop out and stare, and then run in again, like frightened rabbits in a warren.

OMNES: No, no.

HARD: You, Diggory, whom I have taken from the barn, are to make a shew at the side-table; and you, Roger, whom I have advanced from the plough, are to place yourself behind *my* chair. But you're not to stand so, with your hands in your pockets. Take your hands from your pockets, Roger; and from your head, you blockhead you. See how Diggory carries his hands. They're a little too stiff, indeed, but that's no great matter.

DIG: Ay, mind how I hold them. I learned to hold my hands this way, when I was upon drill for the militia. And so being upon drill——

HARD: You must not be so talkative, Diggory. You must be all attention to the guests. You must hear us talk, and not think of talking; you must see us drink, and not think of drinking—you must see us eat, and not think of eating.

DIG: By the laws, your worship, that's parfectly unpossible. Whenever Diggory sees yeating going forward, ecod he's always wishing for a mouthful himself.

HARD: Blockhead! Is not a belly-full in the kitchen as good as a belly-full in the parlour? Stay your stomach with that reflection.

DIG: Ecod I thank your worship, I'll make a shift to stay my stomach with a slice of cold beef in the pantry.

HARD: Diggory, you are too talkative. Then if I happen to say a good thing, or tell a good story at table, you must not all burst out a-laughing, as if you made part of the company.

DIG: Then ecod your worship must not tell the story of Ould Grouse in the gun-room: I can't help laughing at that—he! he! he!—for the soul of me. We have laughed at that these twenty years—ha! ha! ha!

HARD: Ha! ha! ha! The story is a good one. Well, honest Diggory, you may laugh at that—but still remember to be attentive. Suppose one of the company should call for a glass of wine, how will you behave? A glass of wine, Sir, if you please (To DIGGORY)—Eh, why don't you move.

DIG: Ecod your worship, I never have courage till I see the eatables and drinkables brought upo' the table, and then I'm as bauld as a lion.

HARD: What, will no body move?

FIRST SERV: I'm not to leave this pleace.

SECOND SERV: I'm sure it's no pleace of mine.

THIRD SERV: Nor mine, for sartain.

DIG: Wauns, and I'm sure it canna be mine.

HARD: You numskulls! and so while, like your betters, you are quarrelling for places, the guests must be starved. O you dunces! I find I must begin all over again. But don't I hear a coach drive into the yard? To your posts, you blockheads. I'll go in the mean time and give my old friend's son a hearty reception at the gate.

[*Exit* HARDCASTLE

15

DIG: By the elevens, my pleace is gone quite out of my head.

ROGER: I know that my pleace is to be every where.

FIRST SERV: Where the devil is mine?

SECOND SERV: My pleace is to be no where at all; and so Ize go about my business. [*Exeunt* SERVANTS, *running about as if frighted, different ways*

Enter SERVANT *with candles, shewing in* MARLOW *and* HASTINGS

SERV: Welcome, gentlemen, very welcome! This way.

HAST: After the disappointments of the day, welcome once more, Charles, to the comforts of a clean room and a good fire. Upon my word, a very well-looking house; antique, but creditable.

MARL: The usual fate of a large mansion. Having first ruined the master by good housekeeping, it at last comes to levy contributions as an inn.

HAST: As you say, passengers are to be taxed to pay all these fineries. I have often seen a good side-board, or a marble chimney-piece, tho' not actually put in the bill, inflame a reckoning confoundedly.

MARL: Travellers, George, must pay in all places: the only difference is, that in good inns, you pay dearly for luxuries; in bad inns, you are fleeced and starved.

HAST: You have lived pretty much among them. In truth, I have been often surprised, that you who have seen so much of the world, with your natural good sense, and your many opportunities, could never yet acquire a requisite share of assurance.

MARL: The Englishman's malady. But tell me, George, where could I have learned that assurance you talk of? My life has been chiefly spent in a college, or an inn, in seclusion from that lovely part of the creation that chiefly teach men confidence. I don't know that I was ever

familiarly acquainted with a single modest woman—
except my mother—But among females of another class
you know——

HAST: Ay, among them you are impudent enough of all
conscience.

MARL: They are of *us*, you know.

HAST: But in the company of women of reputation I never
saw such an ideot, such a trembler; you look for all the
world as if you wanted an opportunity of stealing out of
the room.

MARL: Why man that's because I *do* want to steal out of
the room. Faith, I have often formed a resolution to break
the ice, and rattle away at any rate. But I don't know
how, a single glance from a pair of fine eyes has totally
overset my resolution. An impudent fellow may counterfeit modesty, but I'll be hanged if a modest man can ever
counterfeit impudence.

HAST: If you could but say half the fine things to them that
I have heard you lavish upon the barmaid of an inn, or
even a college bed maker——

MARL: Why, George, I can't say fine things to them. They
freeze, they petrify me. They may talk of a comet, or a
burning mountain, or some such bagatelle. But to me, a
modest woman, drest out in all her finery, is the most
tremendous object of the whole creation.

HAST: Ha! ha! ha! At this rate, man, how can you ever
expect to marry?

MARL: Never, unless as among kings and princes, my bride
were to be courted by proxy. If, indeed, like an Eastern
bridegroom, one were to be introduced to a wife he never
saw before, it might be endured. But to go through all
the terrors of a formal courtship, together with the
episode of aunts, grandmothers and cousins, and at last to
blurt out the broad staring question of, '*Madam, will you
marry me?*' No, no, that's a strain much above me I
assure you.

HAST: I pity you. But how do you intend behaving to the lady you are come down to visit at the request of your father?

MARL: As I behave to all other ladies. Bow very low. Answer yes, or no, to all her demands—But for the rest, I don't think I shall venture to look in her face, till I see my father's again.

HAST: I'm surprised that one who is so warm a friend can be so cool a lover.

MARL: To be explicit, my dear Hastings, my chief inducement down was to be instrumental in forwarding your happiness, not my own. Miss Neville loves you, the family don't know you, as my friend you are sure of a reception, and let honour do the rest.

HAST: My dear Marlow! But I'll suppress the emotion. Were I a wretch, meanly seeking to carry off a fortune, you should be the last man in the world I would apply to for assistance. But Miss Neville's person is all I ask, and that is mine, both from her deceased father's consent, and her own inclination.

MARL: Happy man! You have talents and art to captivate any woman. I'm doom'd to adore the sex, and yet to converse with the only part of it I despise. This stammer in my address, and this aukward prepossessing visage of mine, can never permit me to soar above the reach of a milliner's 'prentice, or one of the duchesses of Drury-lane. Pshaw! this fellow here to interrupt us!

Enter HARDCASTLE

HARD: Gentlemen, once more you are heartily welcome. Which is Mr. Marlow? Sir, you're heartily welcome. It's not my way, you see, to receive my friends with my back to the fire. I like to give them a hearty reception in the old style at my gate. I like to see their horses and trunks taken care of.

MARL (*Aside*): He has got our names from the servants already. (*To him*) We approve your caution and hospitality, Sir. (*To* HASTINGS) I have been thinking, George, of changing our travelling dresses in the morning. I am grown confoundedly ashamed of mine.

HARD: I beg, Mr. Marlow, you'll use no ceremony in this house.

HAST: I fancy, Charles, you're right: the first blow is half the battle. I intend opening the campaign with the white and gold.

HARD: Mr. Marlow—Mr. Hastings—gentlemen—pray be under no constraint in this house. This is Liberty-hall, gentlemen. You may do just as you please here.

MARL: Yet, George, if we open the campaign too fiercely at first, we may want ammunition before it is over. I think to reserve the embroidery to secure a retreat.

HARD: Your talking of a retreat, Mr. Marlow, puts me in mind of the Duke of Marlborough, when we went to besiege Denain. He first summoned the garrison——

MARL: Don't you think the *ventre d'or* waistcoat will do with the plain brown?

HARD: He first summoned the garrison, which might consist of about five thousand men——

HAST: I think not: brown and yellow mix very poorly.

HARD: I say, gentlemen, as I was telling you, he summoned the garrison, which might consist of about five thousand men——

MARL: The girls like finery.

HARD: Which might consist of about five thousand men, well appointed with stores, ammunition, and other implements of war. Now, says the Duke of Marlborough, to George Brooks, that stood next to him—You must have heard of George Brooks; I'll pawn my Dukedom, says he, but I take that garrison without spilling a drop of blood. So——

MARL: What, my good friend, if you gave us a glass of

punch in the mean time, it would help us to carry on the siege with vigour.

HARD: Punch, Sir! (*Aside*) This is the most unaccountable kind of modesty I ever met with.

MARL: Yes, Sir, punch. A glass of warm punch, after our journey, will be comfortable. This is Liberty-hall, you know.

HARD: Here's cup, Sir.

MARL (*Aside*): So this fellow, in his Liberty-hall, will only let us have just what he pleases.

HARD (*Taking the cup*): I hope you'll find it to your mind. I have prepared it with my own hands, and I believe you'll own the ingredients are tolerable. Will you be so good as to pledge me, Sir? Here, Mr. Marlow, here is to our better acquaintance. (*Drinks*)

MARL (*Aside*): A very impudent fellow this! but he's a character, and I'll humour him a little. Sir, my service to you. (*Drinks*)

HAST (*Aside*): I see this fellow wants to give us his company, and forgets that he's an innkeeper, before he has learned to be a gentleman.

MARL: From the excellence of your cup, my old friend, I suppose you have a good deal of business in this part of the country. Warm work, now and then, at elections, I suppose.

HARD: No, Sir. I have long given that work over. Since our betters have hit upon the expedient of electing each other, there is no business *for us that sell ale*.

HAST: So, then you have no turn for politics I find.

HARD: Not in the least. There was a time, indeed, I fretted myself about the mistakes of government, like other people; but finding myself every day grow more angry, and the government growing no better, I left it to mend itself. Since that, I no more trouble my head about *Heyder Ally*, or *Ally Cawn*, than about *Ally Croaker*. Sir, my service to you.

HAST: So that with eating above stairs, and drinking below, with receiving your friends within, and amusing them without, you lead a good, pleasant bustling life of it.

HARD: I do stir about a great deal, that's certain. Half the differences of the parish are adjusted in this very parlour.

MARL (*After drinking*): And you have an argument in your cup, old gentleman, better than any in Westminster-hall.

HARD: Ay, young gentleman, that, and a little philosophy.

MARL (*Aside*): Well, this is the first time I ever heard of an innkeeper's philosophy.

HAST: So then, like an experienced general, you attack them on every quarter. If you find their reason manageable, you attack it with your philosophy; if you find they have no reason, you attack them with this. Here's your health, my philosopher. (*Drinks*)

HARD: Good, very good, thank you; ha! ha! ha! Your generalship puts me in mind of Prince Eugene, when he fought the Turks at the battle of Belgrade. You shall hear.

MARL: Instead of the battle of Belgrade, I believe it's almost time to talk about supper. What has your philosophy got in the house for supper?

HARD: For supper, Sir! (*Aside*) Was ever such a request to a man in his own house!

MARL: Yes, Sir, supper Sir. I begin to feel an appetite. I shall make devilish work to-night in the larder, I promise you.

HARD (*Aside*): Such a brazen dog sure never my eyes beheld. (*To him*) Why really, Sir, as for supper I can't well tell. My Dorothy, and the cook maid, settle these things between them. I leave these kind of things entirely to them.

MARL: You do, do you?

HARD: Entirely. By-the-bye, I believe they are in actual consultation upon what's for supper this moment in the kitchen.

MARL: Then I beg they'll admit *me* as one of their privy council. It's a way I have got. When I travel I always chuse to regulate my own supper. Let the cook be called. No offence I hope, Sir.

HARD: O no, Sir, none in the least; yet I don't know how: our Bridget, the cook maid, is not very communicative upon these occasions. Should we send for her, she might scold us all out of the house.

HAST: Let's see your list of the larder then. I ask it as a favour. I always match my appetite to my bill of fare.

MARL (*To* HARDCASTLE, *who looks at them with surprise*): Sir, he's very right, and it's my way too.

HARD: Sir, you have a right to command here. Here, Roger, bring us the bill of fare for to-night's supper. I believe it's drawn out. Your manner, Mr. Hastings, puts me in mind of my uncle, Colonel Wallop. It was a saying of his, that no man was sure of his supper till he had eaten it.

HAST (*Aside*): All upon the high ropes! His uncle a Colonel! We shall soon hear of his mother being a justice of the peace. But let's hear the bill of fare.

MARL (*Perusing*): What's here? For the first course; for the second course; for the dessert. The devil, Sir, do you think we have brought down the whole Joiners' Company, or the Corporation of Bedford, to eat up such a supper? Two or three little things, clean and comfortable, will do.

HAST: But, let's hear it.

MARL (*Reading*): For the first course at the top, a pig, and pruin sauce.

HAST: Damn your pig, I say.

MARL: And damn your pruin sauce, say I.

HARD: And yet, gentlemen, to men that are hungry, pig, with pruin sauce, is very good eating.

MARL: At the bottom a calf's tongue and brains.

HAST: Let your brains be knock'd out, my good Sir; I don't like them.

MARL: Or you may clap them on a plate by themselves. I do.

HARD (*Aside*): Their impudence confounds me. (*To them*) Gentlemen, you are my guests, make what alterations you please. Is there any thing else you wish to retrench or alter, gentlemen?

MARL: Item. A pork pye, a boiled rabbit and sausages, a Florentine, a shaking pudding, and a dish of tiff—taff—taffety cream.

HAST: Confound your made dishes, I shall be as much at a loss in this house as at a green and yellow dinner at the French ambassador's table. I'm for plain eating.

HARD: I'm sorry, gentlemen, that I have nothing you like, but if there be any thing you have a particular fancy to——

MARL: Why, really, Sir, your bill of fare is so exquisite, that any one part of it is full as good as another. Send us what you please. So much for supper. And now to see that our beds are air'd, and properly taken care of.

HARD: I entreat you'll leave all that to me. You shall not stir a step.

MARL: Leave that to you! I protest, Sir, you must excuse me, I always look to these things myself.

HARD: I must insist, Sir, you'll make yourself easy on that head.

MARL: You see I'm resolv'd on it. (*Aside*) A very troublesome fellow this, as ever I met with.

HARD: Well, Sir, I'm resolved at least to attend you. (*Aside*) This may be modern modesty, but I never saw any thing look so like old-fashioned impudence.

[*Exeunt* MARLOW *and* HARDCASTLE

HAST (*Solus*): So I find this fellow's civilities begin to grow troublesome. But who can be angry at those assiduities which are meant to please him? Ha! what do I see? Miss Neville, by all that's happy!

Enter MISS NEVILLE

MISS NEV: My dear Hastings! To what unexpected good fortune? to what accident am I to ascribe this happy meeting?

HAST: Rather let me ask the same question, as I could never have hoped to meet my dearest Constance at an inn.

MISS NEV: An inn! sure you mistake! my aunt, my guardian, lives here. What could induce you to think this house an inn?

HAST: My friend, Mr. Marlow, with whom I came down, and I, have been sent here as to an inn, I assure you. A young fellow whom we accidentally met at a house hard by directed us hither.

MISS NEV: Certainly it must be one of my hopeful cousin's tricks, of whom you have heard me talk so often, ha! ha! ha! ha!

HAST: He whom your aunt intends for you? He of whom I have such just apprehensions?

MISS NEV: You have nothing to fear from him, I assure you. You'd adore him if you knew how heartily he despises me. My aunt knows it too, and has undertaken to court me for him, and actually begins to think she has made a conquest.

HAST: Thou dear dissembler! You must know, my Constance, I have just seized this happy opportunity of my friend's visit here to get admittance into the family. The horses that carried us down are now fatigued with their journey, but they'll soon be refreshed; and then if my dearest girl will trust in her faithful Hastings, we shall soon be landed in France, where even among slaves the laws of marriage are respected.

MISS NEV: I have often told you, that though ready to obey you, I yet should leave my little fortune behind with reluctance. The greatest part of it was left me by my uncle, the India Director, and chiefly consists in jewels. I have been for some time persuading my aunt to let me wear them. I fancy I'm very near succeeding. The instant they are put into my possession you shall find me ready to make them and myself yours.

HAST: Perish the baubles! Your person is all I desire. In the meantime, my friend Marlow must not be let into his mistake. I know the strange reserve of his temper is such, that if abruptly informed of it, he would instantly quit the house before our plan was ripe for execution.

MISS NEV: But how shall we keep him in the deception? Miss Hardcastle is just returned from walking; what if we still continue to deceive him?——This, this way——

[*They confer*

Enter MARLOW

MARL: The assiduities of these good people teize me beyond bearing. My host seems to think it ill manners to leave me alone, and so he claps not only himself but his old-fashioned wife on my back. They talk of coming to sup with us too; and then, I suppose, we are to run the gauntlet thro' all the rest of the family.—What have we got here!

HAST: My dear Charles! Let me congratulate you!—The most fortunate accident!—Who do you think is just alighted?

MARL: Cannot guess.

HAST: Our mistresses, boy, Miss Hardcastle and Miss Neville. Give me leave to introduce Miss Constance Neville to your acquaintance. Happening to dine in the neighbourhood, they called, on their return to take fresh horses, here. Miss Hardcastle has just stept into the next room, and will be back in an instant. Wasn't it lucky? eh!

MARL (*Aside*): I have been mortified enough of all conscience, and here comes something to complete my embarrassment.

HAST: Well, but wasn't it the most fortunate thing in the world?

MARL: Oh! yes. Very fortunate—a most joyful encounter —But our dresses, George, you know, are in disorder— What if we should postpone the happiness 'till to-morrow?—To-morrow at her own house—It will be every bit as convenient—And rather more respectful— To-morrow let it be.   [*Offering to go*

MISS NEV: By no means, Sir. Your ceremony will displease her. The disorder of your dress will shew the ardour of your impatience. Besides, she knows you are in the house, and will permit you to see her.

MARL: O! the devil! how shall I support it? Hem! hem! Hastings, you must not go. You are to assist me, you know. I shall be confoundedly ridiculous. Yet, hang it! I'll take courage. Hem!

HAST: Pshaw man! it's but the first plunge, and all's over. She's but a woman, you know.

MARL: And of all women, she that I dread most to encounter.

Enter MISS HARDCASTLE, *as returned from walking, a Bonnet, &c.*

HAST (*introducing them*): Miss Hardcastle, Mr. Marlow. I'm proud of bringing two persons of such merit together, that only want to know, to esteem each other.

MISS HARD (*Aside*): Now, for meeting my modest gentle-man with a demure face, and quite in his own manner. (*After a pause, in which he appears very uneasy and disconcerted*) I'm glad of your safe arrival, Sir—I'm told you had some accidents by the way.

MARL: Only a few, Madam. Yes, we had some. Yes, Madam, a good many accidents but should be sorry—Madam—or rather glad of any accidents—that are so agreeably concluded. Hem!

HAST (*To him*): You never spoke better in your whole life.

Keep it up, and I'll insure you the victory.

MISS HARD: I'm afraid you flatter, Sir. You that have seen so much of the finest company can find little entertainment in an obscure corner of the country.

MARL (Gathering courage): I have lived, indeed, in the world, Madam: but I have kept very little company. I have been but an observer upon life, Madam, while others were enjoying it.

MISS NEV: But that, I am told, is the way to enjoy it at last.

HAST (To him): Cicero never spoke better. Once more, and you are confirmed in assurance for ever.

MARL (To him): Hem! Stand by me then, and when I'm down, throw in a word or two to set me up again.

MISS HARD: An observer, like you, upon life, were, I fear, disagreeably employed, since you must have had much more to censure than to approve.

MARL: Pardon me, Madam. I was always willing to be amused. The folly of most people is rather an object of mirth than uneasiness.

HAST (To him): Bravo, bravo. Never spoke so well in your whole life. Well! Miss Hardcastle, I see that you and Mr. Marlow are going to be very good company. I believe our being here will but embarrass the interview.

MARL: Not in the least, Mr. Hastings. We like your company of all things. (To him) Zounds! George, sure you won't go? How can you leave us?

HAST: Our presence will but spoil conversation, so we'll retire to the next room. (To him) You don't consider, man, that we are to manage a little tête-à-tête of our own.   [Exeunt

MISS HARD (After a pause): But you have not been wholly an observer, I presume, Sir: the ladies I should hope have employed some part of your addresses.

MARL (Relapsing into timidity): Pardon me, Madam, I—I—I—as yet have studied—only—to—deserve them.

MISS HARD: And that, some say, is the very worst way

to obtain them.

MARL: Perhaps so, Madam. But I love to converse only with the more grave and sensible part of the sex.—But I'm afraid I grow tiresome.

MISS HARD: Not at all, Sir; there is nothing I like so much as grave conversation myself; I could hear it for ever. Indeed I have often been surprised how a man of *sentiment* could ever admire those light airy pleasures, where nothing reaches the heart.

MARL: It's——a disease——of the mind, Madam. In the variety of tastes there must be some who wanting a relish for——um——um—a—um.

MISS HARD: I understand you, Sir. There must be some, who, wanting a relish for refined pleasures, pretend to despise what they are incapable of tasting.

MARL: My meaning, Madam, but infinitely better expressed. And I can't help observing——a——

MISS HARD (*Aside*): Who could ever suppose this fellow impudent upon some occasions. (*To him*) You were going to observe, Sir——

MARL: I was observing, Madam—I protest, Madam, I forget what I was going to observe.

MISS HARD (*Aside*): I vow and so do I. (*To him*) You were observing, Sir, that in this age of hypocrisy—something about hypocrisy, Sir.

MARL: Yes, Madam. In this age of hypocrisy there are few who upon strict enquiry do not—a—a—a—

MISS HARD: I understand you perfectly, Sir.

MARL (*Aside*): Egad! and that's more than I do myself.

MISS HARD: You mean that in this hypocritical age there are few that do not condemn in public what they practise in private, and think they pay every debt to virtue when they praise it.

MARL: True, Madam; those who have most virtue in their mouths, have least of it in their bosoms. But I'm sure I tire you, Madam.

MISS HARD: Not in the least, Sir; there's something so agreeable and spirited in your manner, such life and force—pray, Sir, go on.

MARL: Yes, Madam, I was saying——that there are some occasions—when a total want of courage, Madam, destroys all the——and puts us——upon—a—a—a—

MISS HARD: I agree with you entirely, a want of courage upon some occasions assumes the appearance of ignorance, and betrays us when we most want to excel. I beg you'll proceed.

MARL: Yes, Madam. Morally speaking, Madam—But I see Miss Neville expecting us in the next room. I would not intrude for the world.

MISS HARD: I protest, Sir, I never was more agreeably entertained in all my life. Pray go on.

MARL: Yes, Madam, I was—But she beckons us to join her. Madam, shall I do myself the honour to attend you?

MISS HARD: Well then, I'll follow.

MARL (*Aside*): This pretty smooth dialogue has done for me.   [*Exit*

MISS HARD (*Sola*): Ha! ha! ha! Was there ever such a sober sentimental interview? I'm certain he scarce look'd in my face the whole time. Yet the fellow, but for his unaccountable bashfulness, is pretty well too. He has good sense, but then so buried in his fears, that it fatigues one more than ignorance. If I could teach him a little confidence, it would be doing somebody that I know of a piece of service. But who is that somebody?—that, faith, is a question I can scarce answer.   [*Exit*

Enter TONY and MISS NEVILLE, *followed by* MRS.
HARDCASTLE *and* HASTINGS

TONY: What do you follow me for, cousin Con? I wonder you're not ashamed to be so very engaging.

MISS NEV: I hope, cousin, one may speak to one's own relations, and not be to blame.

TONY: Ay, but I know what sort of a relation you want to make me, though; but it won't do. I tell you, cousin Con, it won't do, so I beg you'll keep your distance, I want no nearer relationship.

[*She follows coquetting him to the back scene*

MRS. HARD: Well! I vow, Mr. Hastings, you are very entertaining. There is nothing in the world I love to talk of so much as London, and the fashions, though I was never there myself.

HAST: Never there! You amaze me! From your air and manner, I concluded you had been bred all your life either at Ranelagh, St. James's, or Tower Wharf.

MRS. HARD: O! Sir, you're only pleased to say so. We country persons can have no manner at all. I'm in love with the town, and that serves to raise me above some of our neighbouring rustics; but who can have a manner, that has never seen the Pantheon, the Grotto Gardens, the Borough, and such places where the Nobility chiefly resort? All I can do is to enjoy London at second-hand. I take care to know every tête-à-tête from the Scandalous Magazine, and have all the fashions, as they come out, in a letter from the two Miss Rickets of Crooked-lane. Pray how do you like this head, Mr. Hastings?

HAST: Extremely elegant and dégagée, upon my word, Madam. Your friseur is a Frenchman, I suppose?

MRS. HARD: I protest I dressed it myself from a print in the Ladies' Memorandum-book for the last year.

HAST: Indeed! Such a head in a side-box, at the Playhouse, would draw as many gazers as my Lady May'ress at a City Ball.

MRS. HARD: I vow, since inoculation began, there is no such thing to be seen as a plain woman; so one must dress a little particular or one may escape in the crowd.

HAST: But that can never be your case, Madam, in any dress. (*Bowing*)

MRS. HARD: Yet, what signifies *my* dressing when I have

such a piece of antiquity by my side as Mr. Hardcastle: all I can say will never argue down a single button from his cloaths. I have often wanted him to throw off his great flaxen wig, and where he was bald, to plaister it over, like my Lord Pately, with powder.

HAST: You are right, Madam; for, as among the ladies there are none ugly, so among the men there are none old.

MRS. HARD: But what do you think his answer was? Why, with his usual Gothic vivacity, he said I only wanted him to throw off his wig to convert it into a tête for my own wearing.

HAST: Intolerable! At your age you may wear what you please, and it must become you.

MRS. HARD: Pray, Mr. Hastings, what do you take to be the most fashionable age about town?

HAST: Some time ago, forty was all the mode; but I'm told the ladies intend to bring up fifty for the ensuing winter.

MRS. HARD: Seriously? Then I shall be too young for the fashion.

HAST: No lady begins now to put on jewels 'till she's past forty. For instance, Miss there, in a polite circle, would be considered as a child, as a mere maker of samplers.

MRS. HARD: And yet Mrs. Niece thinks herself as much a woman, and is as fond of jewels as the oldest of us all.

HAST: Your niece, is she? And that young gentleman, a brother of yours, I should presume?

MRS. HARD: My son, Sir. They are contracted to each other. Observe their little sports. They fall in and out ten times a day, as if they were man and wife already. (To them) Well Tony, child, what soft things are you saying to your cousin Constance this evening?

TONY: I have been saying no soft things; but that it's very hard to be followed about so. Ecod! I've not a place in the house now that's left to myself but the stable.

MRS. HARD: Never mind him, Con, my dear. He's in another story behind your back.

MISS NEV: There's something generous in my cousin's manner. He falls out before faces to be forgiven in private.

TONY: That's a damned confounded—crack.

MRS. HARD: Ah! he's a sly one. Don't you think they're like each other about the mouth, Mr. Hastings? The Blenkinsop mouth to a T. They're of a size too. Back to back, my pretties, that Mr. Hastings may see you. Come Tony.

TONY: You had as good not make me, I tell you.

(Measuring)

MISS NEV: O lud! he has almost cracked my head.

MRS. HARD: O the monster! For shame, Tony. You a man, and behave so!

TONY: If I'm a man, let me have my fortin. Ecod! I'll not be made a fool of no longer.

MRS. HARD: Is this, ungrateful boy, all that I'm to get for the pains I have taken in your education? I that have rock'd you in your cradle, and fed that pretty mouth with a spoon! Did I not work that waistcoat to make you genteel? Did I not prescribe for you every day, and weep while the receipt was operating?

TONY: Ecod! You had reason to weep, for you have been dosing me ever since I was born. I have gone through every receipt in the compleat huswife ten times over; and you have thoughts of coursing me through Quincy next spring. But, ecod! I tell you, I'll not be made a fool of no longer.

MRS. HARD: Wasn't it all for your good, viper? Wasn't it all for your good?

TONY: I wish you'd let me and my good alone then. Snubbing this way when I'm in spirits. If I'm to have any good, let it come of itself; not to keep dinging it, dinging it into one so.

MRS. HARD: That's false; I never see you when you're in spirits. No, Tony, you then go to the alehouse or kennel.

I'm never to be delighted with your agreeable, wild notes, unfeeling monster!

TONY: Ecod! Mama, your own notes are the wildest of the two.

MRS. HARD: Was ever the like? But I see he wants to break my heart, I see he does.

HAST: Dear Madam, permit me to lecture the young gentleman a little. I'm certain I can persuade him to his duty.

MRS. HARD: Well! I must retire. Come, Constance, my love. You see Mr. Hastings, the wretchedness of my situation: Was ever poor woman so plagued with a dear, sweet, pretty, provoking, undutiful boy.

[*Exeunt* MRS. HARDCASTLE *and* MISS NEVILLE

HASTINGS, TONY

TONY (*Singing*) *There was a young man riding by and fain would have his will. Rang do didlo dee.*—Don't mind her. Let her cry. It's the comfort of her heart. I have seen her and sister cry over a book for an hour together, and they said, they liked the book the better the more it made them cry.

HAST: Then you're no friend to the ladies, I find, my pretty young gentleman?

TONY: That's as I find 'um.

HAST: Not to her of your mother's chusing, I dare answer? And yet she appears to me a pretty well-tempered girl.

TONY: That's because you don't know her as well as I. Ecod! I know every inch about her; and there's not a more bitter cantanckerous toad in all Christendom.

HAST (*Aside*): Pretty encouragement this for a lover!

TONY: I have seen her since the height of that. She has as many tricks as a hare in a thicket, or a colt the first day's breaking.

HAST: To me she appears sensible and silent.

TONY: Ay, before company. But when she's with her play-mates she's as loud as a hog in a gate.

HAST: But there is a meek modesty about her that charms me.

TONY: Yes, but curb her never so little, she kicks up, and you're flung in a ditch.

HAST: Well, but you must allow her a little beauty.—Yes, you must allow her some beauty.

TONY: Bandbox! She's all a made-up thing, mun. Ah! could you but see Bett Bouncer of these parts, you might then talk of beauty. Ecod, she has two eyes as black as sloes, and cheeks as broad and red as a pulpit cushion. She'd make two of she.

HAST: Well, what say you to a friend that would take this bitter bargain off your hands?

TONY: Anon.

HAST: Would you thank him that would take Miss Neville and leave you to happiness and your dear Betsy?

TONY: Ay; but where is there such a friend, for who would take *her*?

HAST: I am he. If you but assist me, I'll engage to whip her off to France, and you shall never hear more of her.

TONY: Assist you! Ecod I will, to the last drop of my blood. I'll clap a pair of horses to your chaise that shall trundle you off in a twinkling, and may be get you a part of her fortin beside, in jewels, that you little dream of.

HAST: My dear 'squire, this looks like a lad of spirit.

TONY: Come along then, and you shall see more of my spirit before you have done with me. (*Singing*) *We are the boys, That fears no noise, Where the thundering cannons roar.*

[*Exeunt*

ACT III

Enter HARDCASTLE, solus

HARD: What could my old friend Sir Charles mean by recommending his son as the modestest young man in town? To me he appears the most impudent piece of brass that ever spoke with a tongue. He has taken possession of the easy chair by the fire-side already. He took off his boots in the parlour, and desired me to see them taken care of. I'm desirous to know how his impudence affects my daughter.—She will certainly be shocked at it.

Enter MISS HARDCASTLE, plainly dressed

HARD: Well, my Kate, I see you have changed your dress as I bid you; and yet, I believe, there was no great occasion.

MISS HARD: I find such a pleasure, Sir, in obeying your commands, that I take care to observe them without ever debating their propriety.

HARD: And yet, Kate, I sometimes give you some cause, particularly when I recommended my *modest* gentleman to you as a lover to-day.

MISS HARD: You taught me to expect something extraordinary, and I find the original exceeds the description.

HARD: I was never so surprised in my life! He has quite confounded all my faculties!

MISS HARD: I never saw any thing like it: And a man of the world too!

HARD: Ay, he learned it all abroad—what a fool was I, to think a young man could learn modesty by travelling. He might as soon learn wit at a masquerade.

MISS HARD: It seems all natural to him.

HARD: A good deal assisted by bad company and a French dancing-master.

MISS HARD: Sure you mistake, Papa! a French dancing-master could never have taught him that timid look, that aukward address, that bashful manner—

HARD: Whose look? Whose manner? child!

MISS HARD: Mr. Marlow's: his *mauvaise honte*, his timidity struck me at the first sight.

HARD: Then your first sight deceived you; for I think him one of the most brazen first sights that ever astonished my senses.

MISS HARD: Sure, Sir, you rally! I never saw any one so modest.

HARD: And can you be serious! I never saw such a bouncing, swaggering puppy since I was born. Bully Dawson was but a fool to him.

MISS HARD: Surprising! He met me with a respectful bow, a stammering voice, and a look fixed on the ground.

HARD: He met me with a loud voice, a lordly air, and a familiarity that made my blood freeze again.

MISS HARD: He treated me with diffidence and respect; censured the manners of the age; admired the prudence of girls that never laughed; tired me with apologies for being tiresome; then left the room with a bow, and, Madam, I would not for the world detain you.

HARD: He spoke to me as if he knew me all his life before. Asked twenty questions, and never waited for an answer. Interrupted my best remarks with some silly pun, and when I was in my best story of the Duke of Marlborough and Prince Eugene, he asked if I had not a good hand at making punch. Yes, Kate, he asked your father if he was a maker of punch.

MISS HARD: One of us must certainly be mistaken.

HARD: If he be what he has shewn himself, I'm determined he shall never have my consent.

MISS HARD: And if he be the sullen thing I take him, he

shall never have mine.

HARD: In one thing then we are agreed—to reject him.

MISS HARD: Yes. But upon conditions. For if you should find him less impudent, and I more presuming; if you find him more respectful, and I more importunate——I don't know——the fellow is well enough for a man— Certainly we don't meet many such at a horse race in the country.

HARD: If we should find him so——But that's impossible. The first appearance has done my business. I'm seldom deceived in that.

MISS HARD: And yet there may be many good qualities under that first appearance.

HARD: Ay, when a girl finds a fellow's outside to her taste, she then sets about guessing the rest of his furniture. With her, a smooth face stands for good sense, and a genteel figure for every virtue.

MISS HARD: I hope, Sir, a conversation begun with a compliment to my good sense won't end with a sneer at my understanding?

HARD: Pardon me, Kate. But if young Mr. Brazen can find the art of reconciling contradictions, he may please us both, perhaps.

MISS HARD: And as one of us must be mistaken, what if we go to make further discoveries?

HARD: Agreed. But depend on 't I'm in the right.

MISS HARD: And depend on 't I'm not much in the wrong.

[*Exeunt*

Enter TONY, *running in with a casket*

TONY: Ecod! I have got them. Here they are. My cousin Con's necklaces, bobs and all. My mother shan't cheat the poor souls out of their fortin neither. O! my genus, is that you?

37

Enter HASTINGS

HAST: My dear friend, how have you managed with your mother? I hope you have amused her with pretending love for your cousin, and that you are willing to be reconciled at last? Our horses will be refreshed in a short time, and we shall soon be ready to set off.

TONY: And here's something to bear your charges by the way (*giving the casket*). Your sweetheart's jewels. Keep them, and hang those, I say, that would rob you of one of them.

HAST: But how have you procured them from your mother?

TONY: Ask me no questions, and I'll tell you no fibs. I procured them by the rule of thumb. If I had not a key to every drawer in mother's bureau, how could I go to the alehouse so often as I do. An honest man may rob himself of his own at any time.

HAST: Thousands do it every day. But to be plain with you; Miss Neville is endeavouring to procure them from her aunt this very instant. If she succeeds, it will be the most delicate way at least of obtaining them.

TONY: Well, keep them, till you know how it will be. But I know how it will be well enough, she'd as soon part with the only sound tooth in her head.

HAST: But I dread the effects of her resentment, when she finds she has lost them.

TONY: Never you mind her resentment, leave me to manage that. I don't value her resentment the bounce of a cracker. Zounds! here they are. Morrice. Prance.

[*Exit* HASTINGS

TONY, MRS. HARDCASTLE, *and* MISS NEVILLE

MRS. HARD: Indeed, Constance, you amaze me. Such a girl as you want jewels? It will be time enough for jewels, my dear, twenty years hence, when your beauty begins to want repairs.

MISS NEV: But what will repair beauty at forty, will certainly improve it at twenty, Madam.

MRS. HARD: Yours, my dear, can admit of none. That natural blush is beyond a thousand ornaments. Besides, child, jewels are quite out at present. Don't you see half the ladies of our acquaintance, my lady Kill-day-light, and Mrs. Crump, and the rest of them carry their jewels to town, and bring nothing but paste and marcasites back.

MISS NEV: But who knows, Madam, but somebody that shall be nameless would like me best with all my little finery about me?

MRS. HARD: Consult your glass, my dear, and then see if, with such a pair of eyes, you want any better sparklers. What do you think, Tony, my dear, does your cousin Con want any jewels in your eyes to set off her beauty?

TONY: That's as thereafter may be.

MISS NEV: My dear aunt, if you knew how it would oblige me.

MRS. HARD: A parcel of old-fashioned rose and table-cut things. They would make you look like the court of king Solomon at a puppet-shew. Besides, I believe I can't readily come at them. They may be missing for aught I know to the contrary.

TONY (*Apart to* MRS. HARDCASTLE): Then why don't you tell her so at once, as she's so longing for them? Tell her they're lost. It's the only way to quiet her. Say they're lost, and call me to bear witness.

MRS. HARD (*Apart to* TONY): You know, my dear, I'm only keeping them for you. So if I say they're gone, you'll bear me witness, will you? He! he! he!

TONY: Never fear me. Ecod! I'll say I saw them taken out with my own eyes.

MISS NEV: I desire them but for a day, Madam. Just to be permitted to shew them as relics, and then they may be lock'd up again.

MRS. HARD: To be plain with you, my dear Constance; if I could find them, you should have them. They're missing, I assure you. Lost, for aught I know; but we must have patience wherever they are.

MISS NEV: I'll not believe it; this is but a shallow pretence to deny me. I know they're too valuable to be so slightly kept, and as you are to answer for the loss.

MRS. HARD: Don't be alarm'd, Constance. If they be lost, I must restore an equivalent. But my son knows they are missing, and not to be found.

TONY: That I can bear witness to. They are missing, and not to be found, I'll take my oath on 't.

MRS. HARD: You must learn resignation, my dear; for tho' we lose our fortune, yet we should not lose our patience. See me, how calm I am.

MISS NEV: Ay, people are generally calm at the misfortunes of others.

MRS. HARD: Now, I wonder a girl of your good sense should waste a thought upon such trumpery. We shall soon find them; and, in the mean time, you shall make use of my garnets till your jewels be found.

MISS NEV: I detest garnets.

MRS. HARD: The most becoming things in the world to set off a clear complexion. You have often seen how well they look upon me. You *shall* have them.   [Exit

MISS NEV: I dislike them of all things. You shan't stir.— Was ever any thing so provoking—to mislay my own jewels and force me to wear her trumpery.

TONY: Don't be a fool. If she gives you the garnets, take what you can get. The jewels are your own already. I have stolen them out of her bureau, and she does not know it. Fly to your spark, he'll tell you more of the matter. Leave me to manage *her*.

MISS NEV: My dear cousin !

TONY: Vanish. She's here, and has missed them already.

[*Exit* MISS NEVILLE.] Zounds! how she fidgets and spits about like a Catherine wheel.

Enter MRS. HARDCASTLE

MRS. HARD: Confusion! thieves! robbers! We are cheated, plundered, broke open, undone.

TONY: What's the matter, what's the matter, Mama? I hope nothing has happened to any of the good family!

MRS. HARD: We are robbed. My bureau has been broke open, the jewels taken out, and I'm undone.

TONY: Oh! is that all? Ha, ha, ha. By the laws, I never saw it better acted in my life. Ecod, I thought you was ruin'd in earnest, ha, ha, ha.

MRS. HARD: Why, boy, I *am* ruin'd in earnest. My bureau has been broke open, and all taken away.

TONY: Stick to that; ha, ha, ha; stick to that. I'll bear witness, you know, call me to bear witness.

MRS. HARD: I tell you, Tony, by all that's precious, the jewels are gone, and I shall be ruin'd for ever.

TONY: Sure I know they're gone, and I'm to say so.

MRS. HARD: My dearest Tony, but hear me. They're gone, I say.

TONY: By the laws, Mama, you make me for to laugh, ha, ha. I know who took them well enough, ha, ha, ha.

MRS. HARD: Was there ever such a blockhead, that can't tell the difference between jest and earnest. I tell you I'm not in jest, booby.

TONY: That's right, that's right: You must be in a bitter passion, and then nobody will suspect either of us. I'll bear witness that they are gone.

MRS. HARD: Was there ever such a cross-grain'd brute, that won't hear me! Can you bear witness that you're no better than a fool? Was ever poor woman so beset with fools on one hand, and thieves on the other.

TONY: I can bear witness to that.

MRS. HARD: Bear witness again, you blockhead you, and

I'll turn you out of the room directly. My poor niece,
what will become of *her*! Do you laugh, you unfeeling
brute, as if you enjoy'd my distress?

TONY: I can bear witness to that.

MRS. HARD: Do you insult me, monster? I'll teach you to
vex your mother, I will.

TONY: I can bear witness to that.

[*He runs off, she follows him*

Enter MISS HARDCASTLE *and* MAID

MISS HARD: What an unaccountable creature is that
brother of mine, to send them to the house as an inn, ha,
ha. I don't wonder at his impudence.

MAID: But what is more, Madam, the young gentleman as
you passed by in your present dress, ask'd me if you
were the barmaid? He mistook you for the barmaid,
Madam.

MISS HARD: Did he? Then as I live I'm resolved to keep
up the delusion. Tell me, Pimple, how do you like my
present dress? Don't you think I look something like
Cherry in the Beaux' Stratagem?

MAID: It's the dress, Madam, that every lady wears in the
country, but when she visits or receives company.

MISS HARD: And are you sure he does not remember my
face or person?

MAID: Certain of it.

MISS HARD: I vow I thought so; for though we spoke for
some time together, yet his fears were such, that he never
once looked up during the interview. Indeed, if he had,
my bonnet would have kept him from seeing me.

MAID: But what do you hope from keeping him in his
mistake.

MISS HARD: In the first place, I shall be *seen*, and that is
no small advantage to a girl who brings her face to
market. Then I shall perhaps make an acquaintance, and
that's no small victory gained over one who never

addresses any but the wildest of her sex. But my chief aim is to take my gentleman off his guard, and like an invisible champion of romance examine the giant's force before I offer to combat.

MAID: But are you sure you can act your part, and disguise your voice, so that he may mistake that, as he has already mistaken your person?

MISS HARD: Never fear me. I think I have got the true bar cant—Did your honour call?—Attend the Lion there.— Pipes and tobacco for the Angel.—The Lamb has been outrageous this half hour.

MAID: It will do, Madam. But he's here.   [Exit MAID

Enter MARLOW

MARL: What a bawling in every part of the house; I have scarce a moment's repose. If I go to the best room, there I find my host and his story. If I fly to the gallery, there we have my hostess with her curtesy down to the ground. I have at last got a moment to myself, and now for recollection.   [Walks and muses

MISS HARD: Did you call, Sir? did your honour call?

MARL (Musing): As for Miss Hardcastle, she's too grave and sentimental for me.

MISS HARD: Did your honour call?

        [She still places herself before him, he turning away

MARL: No, child. (Musing) Besides, from the glimpse I had of her, I think she squints.

MISS HARD: I'm sure, Sir, I heard the bell ring.

MARL: No, no. (Musing) I have pleased my father, however, by coming down, and I'll to-morrow please myself by returning.   [Taking out his tablets, and perusing

MISS HARD: Perhaps the other gentleman called, Sir?

MARL: I tell you, no.

MISS HARD: I should be glad to know, Sir. We have such a parcel of servants.

MARL: No, no, I tell you. (Looks full in her face) Yes, child,

I think I did call. I wanted—I wanted—I vow, child, you are vastly handsome.

MISS HARD: O la, Sir, you'll make one asham'd.

MARL: Never saw a more sprightly malicious eye. Yes, yes, my dear, I did call. Have you got any of your—a— what d'ye call it, in the house?

MISS HARD: No, Sir, we have been out of that these ten days.

MARL: One may call in this house, I find, to very little purpose. Suppose I should call for a taste, just by way of trial, of the nectar of your lips; perhaps I might be disappointed in that too.

MISS HARD: Nectar! nectar! that's a liquor there's no call for in these parts. French, I suppose. We keep no French wines here, Sir.

MARL: Of true English growth, I assure you.

MISS HARD: Then it's odd I should not know it. We brew all sorts of wines in this house, and I have lived here these eighteen years.

MARL: Eighteen years! Why one would think, child, you kept the bar before you were born. How old are you?

MISS HARD: O! Sir, I must not tell my age. They say women and music should never be dated.

MARL: To guess at this distance, you can't be much above forty (*approaching*). Yet nearer I don't think so much (*approaching*). By coming close to some women, they look younger still; but when we come very close indeed— (*attempting to kiss her*).

MISS HARD: Pray, Sir, keep your distance. One would think you wanted to know one's age as they do horses, by mark of mouth.

MARL: I protest, child, you use me extremely ill. If you keep me at this distance, how is it possible you and I can ever be acquainted.

MISS HARD: And who wants to be acquainted with you? I want no such acquaintance, not I. I'm sure you did not

treat Miss Hardcastle that was here awhile ago in this
obstropalous manner. I'll warrant me, before her you
look'd dash'd, and kept bowing to the ground, and talk'd,
for all the world, as if you was before a justice of
peace.

MARL (*Aside*): Egad! She has hit it, sure enough. (*To her*)
In awe of her, child? Ha! ha! ha! A mere, aukward,
squinting thing, no, no. I find you don't know me. I
laugh'd and rallied her a little; but I was unwilling
to be too severe. No, I could not be too severe, *curse
me!*

MISS HARD: O! then, Sir, you are a favourite, I find,
among the ladies?

MARL: Yes, my dear, a great favourite. And yet, hang me,
I don't see what they find in me to follow. At the Ladies'
Club in town I'm called their agreeable Rattle. Rattle,
child, is not my real name, but one I'm known by. My
name is Solomons. Mr. Solomons, my dear, at your service.
[*Offering to salute her*

MISS HARD: Hold, Sir; you are introducing me to your club,
not to yourself. And you're so great a favourite there,
you say?

MARL: Yes, my dear. There's Mrs. Mantrap, Lady Betty
Blackleg, the Countess of Sligo, Mrs. Langhorns, old Miss
Biddy Buckskin, and your humble servant, keep up the
spirit of the place.

MISS HARD: Then it's a very merry place, I suppose?

MARL: Yes, as merry as cards, suppers, wine, and old
women can make us.

MISS HARD: And their agreeable Rattle, ha! ha! ha!

MARL (*Aside*): Egad! I don't quite like this chit. She seems
knowing, methinks. You laugh, child!

MISS HARD: I can't but laugh to think what time they all
have for minding their work or their family.

MARL (*Aside*): All's well; she don't laugh at me. (*To her*)
Do you ever work, child?

MISS HARD: Ay, sure. There's not a screen or a quilt in the whole house but what can bear witness to that.

MARL: Odso! Then you must shew me your embroidery. I embroider and draw patterns myself a little. If you want a judge of your work you must apply to me.

[Seizing her hand

MISS HARD: Ay, but the colours do not look well by candle light. You shall see all in the morning.

[Struggling

MARL: And why not now, my angel? Such beauty fires beyond the power of resistance.——Pshaw! the father here! My old luck: I never nick'd seven that I did not throw ames ace three times following.   [Exit MARLOW

Enter HARDCASTLE, who stands in surprise

HARD: So, Madam! So I find this is your modest lover. This is your humble admirer that kept his eyes fixed on the ground, and only ador'd at humble distance. Kate, Kate, art thou not asham'd to deceive your father so.   .

MISS HARD: Never trust me, dear Papa, but he's still the modest man I first took him for, you'll be convinced of it as well as I.

HARD: By the hand of my body, I believe his impudence is infectious! Didn't I see him seize your hand? Didn't I see him hawl you about like a milk maid? and now you talk of his respect and his modesty, forsooth!

MISS HARD: But if I shortly convince you of his modesty, that he has only the faults that will pass off with time, and the virtues that will improve with age, I hope you'll forgive him.

HARD: The girl would actually make one run mad! I tell you I'll not be convinced. I am convinced. He has scarce been three hours in the house, and he has already encroached on all my prerogatives. You may like his impudence, and call it modesty. But my son-in-law, Madam, must have very different qualifications.

MISS HARD: Sir, I ask but this night to convince you.

HARD: You shall not have half the time, for I have thoughts of turning him out this very hour.

MISS HARD: Give me that hour then, and I hope to satisfy you.

HARD: Well, an hour let it be, then. But I'll have no trifling with your father. All fair and open do you mind me.

MISS HARD: I hope, Sir, you have ever found that I considered your commands as my pride; for your kindness is such, that my duty as yet has been inclination.

[*Exeunt*

ACT IV

Enter HASTINGS and MISS NEVILLE

HAST: You surprise me! Sir Charles Marlow expected here this night? Where have you had your information?

MISS NEV: You may depend upon it. I just saw his letter to Mr. Hardcastle, in which he tells him he intends setting out a few hours after his son.

HAST: Then, my Constance, all must be completed before he arrives. He knows me; and should he find me here, would discover my name, and perhaps my designs, to the rest of the family.

MISS NEV: The jewels, I hope, are safe.

HAST: Yes, yes. I have sent them to Marlow, who keeps the keys of our baggage. In the meantime I'll go to prepare matters for our elopement. I have had the Squire's promise of a fresh pair of horses; and, if I should not see him again, will write him further directions.

[*Exit*

MISS NEV: Well! success attend you. In the meantime I'll go amuse my aunt with the old pretence of a violent passion for my cousin. [*Exit*

Enter MARLOW, followed by a SERVANT

MARL: I wonder what Hastings could mean by sending me so valuable a thing as a casket to keep for him, when he knows the only place I have is the seat of a post-coach at an inn-door. Have you deposited the casket with the landlady, as I ordered you? Have you put it into her own hands?

SERV: Yes, your honour.

MARL: She said she'd keep it safe, did she?

SERV: Yes, she said she'd keep it safe enough; she ask'd me

how I came by it? and she said she had a great mind to make me give an account of myself.   [Exit SERVANT

MARL: Ha! ha! ha! They're safe however. What an unaccountable set of beings have we got amongst! This little barmaid though runs in my head most strangely, and drives out the absurdities of all the rest of the family. She's mine, she must be mine, or I'm greatly mistaken.

Enter HASTINGS

HAST: Bless me! I quite forgot to tell her that I intended to prepare at the bottom of the garden. Marlow here, and in spirits too.

MARL: Give me joy, George! Crown me, shadow me with laurels! Well, George, after all, we modest fellows don't want for success among the women.

HAST: Some women, you mean. But what success has your honour's modesty been crowned with now that it grows so insolent upon us?

MARL: Didn't you see the tempting, brisk, lovely, little thing that runs about the house with a bunch of keys to its girdle.

HAST: Well! and what then?

MARL: She's mine, you rogue you. Such fire, such motion, such eyes, such lips—but, egad, she would not let me kiss them though.

HAST: But are you so sure, so very sure of her?

MARL: Why man, she talk'd of shewing me her work above-stairs, and I am to approve the pattern.

HAST: But how can *you*, Charles, go about to rob a woman of her honour?

MARL: Pshaw! pshaw! We all know the honour of the barmaid of an inn. I don't intend to *rob* her, take my word for it, there's nothing in this house, I shan't honestly *pay* for.

HAST: I believe the girl has virtue.

MARL: And if she has, I should be the last man in the world that would attempt to corrupt it.

HAST: You have taken care, I hope, of the casket I sent you to lock up? It's in safety?

MARL: Yes, yes. It's safe enough. I have taken care of it. But how could you think the seat of a post-coach at an inn-door a place of safety? Ah! numskull! I have taken better precautions for you than you did for yourself—— I have——

HAST: What!

MARL: I have sent it to the landlady to keep for you.

HAST: To the landlady!

MARL: The landlady!

HAST: You did?

MARL: I did. She's to be answerable for its forth-coming, you know.

HAST: Yes, she'll bring it forth, with a witness.

MARL: Wasn't I right? I believe you'll allow that I acted prudently upon this occasion?

HAST (Aside): He must not see my uneasiness.

MARL: You seem a little disconcerted though, methinks. Sure nothing has happened?

HAST: No, nothing. Never was in better spirits in all my life. And so you left it with the landlady, who, no doubt, very readily undertook the charge?

MARL: Rather too readily. For she not only kept the casket; but, thro' her great precaution, was going to keep the messenger too. Ha! ha! ha!

HAST: He! he! he! They're safe however.

MARL: As a guinea in a miser's purse.

HAST (Aside): So now all hopes of fortune are at an end, and we must set off without it. (To him) Well, Charles, I'll leave you to your meditations on the pretty barmaid, and, he! he! he! may you be as successful for yourself as you have been for me.   [Exit

MARL: Thank ye, George! I ask no more. Ha! ha! ha!

Enter HARDCASTLE

HARD: I no longer know my own house. It's turned all topsey-turvey. His servants have got drunk already. I'll bear it no longer, and yet, from my respect for his father, I'll be calm. (*To him*) Mr. Marlow; your servant. I'm your very humble servant.   [*Bowing low*

MARL: Sir, your humble servant. (*Aside*) What's to be the wonder now?

HARD: I believe, Sir, you must be sensible, Sir, that no man alive ought to be more welcome than your father's son, Sir. I hope you think so?

MARL: I do from my soul, Sir. I don't want much intreaty. I generally make my father's son welcome wherever he goes.

HARD: I believe you do, from my soul, Sir. But tho' I say nothing to your own conduct, that of your servants is insufferable. Their manner of drinking is setting a very bad example in this house, I assure you.

MARL: I protest, my very good sir, that is no fault of mine. If they don't drink as they ought, *they* are to blame. I ordered them not to spare the cellar. I did, I assure you. (*To the side scene*) Here, let one of my servants come up. (*To him*) My positive directions were, that as I did not drink myself, they should make up for my deficiencies below.

HARD: Then they had your orders for what they do! I'm satisfied.

MARL: They had, I assure. You shall hear from one of themselves.

Enter SERVANT, *drunk*

MARL: You, Jeremy! Come forward, sirrah! What were my orders? Were you not told to drink freely, and call for what you thought fit, for the good of the house?

HARD (*Aside*): I begin to lose my patience.

JER: Please your honour, liberty and Fleet-street for ever! Though I'm but a servant, I'm as good as another man. I'll drink for no man before supper, Sir, dammy! Good liquor will sit upon a good supper, but a good supper will not sit upon——hiccup——upon my conscience, Sir.

MARL: You see, my old friend, the fellow is as drunk as he can possibly be. I don't know what you'd have more, unless you'd have the poor devil soused in a beer-barrel.

HARD: Zounds! he'll drive me distracted if I contain myself any longer. Mr. Marlow. Sir; I have submitted to your insolence for more than four hours, and I see no likelihood of its coming to an end. I'm now resolved to be master here, Sir, and I desire that you and your drunken pack may leave my house directly.

MARL: Leave your house!——Sure you jest, my good friend? What, when I'm doing what I can to please you.

HARD: I tell you, Sir, you don't please me; so I desire you'll leave my house.

MARL: Sure you cannot be serious? At this time o' night, and such a night. You only mean to banter me?

HARD: I tell you, Sir, I'm serious; and, now that my passions are roused, I say this house is mine, Sir; this house is mine, and I command you to leave it directly.

MARL: Ha! ha! ha! A puddle in a storm. I shan't stir a step, I assure you. (*In a serious tone*) This your house, fellow! It's my house. This is my house. Mine, while I chuse to stay. What right have you to bid me leave this house, Sir? I never met with such impudence, curse me, never in my whole life before.

HARD: Nor I, confound me if ever I did. To come to my house, to call for what he likes, to turn me out of my own chair, to insult the family, to order his servants to get drunk, and then to tell me *This house is mine, Sir.*

By all that's impudent, it makes me laugh. Ha! ha! ha! Pray, Sir, (*bantering*) as you take the house, what think you of taking the rest of the furniture? There's a pair of silver candlesticks, and there's a fire-screen, and here's a pair of brazen-nosed bellows, perhaps you may take a fancy to them?

MARL: Bring me your bill, Sir, bring me your bill, and let's make no more words about it.

HARD: There are a set of prints too. What think you of the Rake's Progress for your own apartment?

MARL: Bring me your bill, I say; and I'll leave you and your infernal house directly.

HARD: Then there's a mahogany table that you may see your own face in.

MARL: My bill, I say.

HARD: I had forgot the great chair, for your own particular slumbers, after a hearty meal.

MARL: Zounds! bring me my bill, I say, and let's hear no more on 't.

HARD: Young man, young man, from your father's letter to me, I was taught to expect a well-bred modest man, as a visitor here, but now I find him no better than a coxcomb and a bully; but he will be down here presently, and shall hear more of it.   [*Exit*

MARL: How's this! Sure I have not mistaken the house. Every thing looks like an inn. The servants cry 'Coming!' The attendance is aukward; the barmaid too to attend us. But she's here, and will further inform me. Whither so fast, child. A word with you.

Enter MISS HARDCASTLE

MISS HARD: Let it be short then. I'm in a hurry. (*Aside*) I believe he begins to find out his mistake, but it's too soon quite to undeceive him.

MARL: Pray, child, answer me one question. What are you, and what may your business in this house be?

MISS HARD: A relation of the family, Sir.

MARL: What. A poor relation?

MISS HARD: Yes, Sir. A poor relation appointed to keep the keys, and to see that the guests want nothing in my power to give them.

MARL: That is, you act as the barmaid of this inn.

MISS HARD: Inn. O law——What brought that in your head? One of the best families in the county keep an inn? Ha, ha, ha, old Mr. Hardcastle's house an inn!

MARL: Mr. Hardcastle's house! Is this Mr. Hardcastle's house, child?

MISS HARD: Ay, sure. Whose else should it be?

MARL: So then all's out, and I have been damnably imposed on. O, confound my stupid head, I shall be laugh'd at over the whole town, I shall be stuck up in caricatura in all the print shops—The *Dullissimo-Maccaroni*. To mistake this house of all others for an inn, and my father's old friend for an inn-keeper! What a swaggering puppy must he take me for! What a silly puppy do I find myself! There again, may I be hang'd, my dear, but I mistook you for the barmaid.

MISS HARD: Dear me! dear me! I'm sure there's nothing in my *behaviour* to put me upon a level with one of that stamp.

MARL: Nothing, my dear, nothing. But I was in for a list of blunders and could not help making you a subscriber. My stupidity saw every thing the wrong way. I mistook your assiduity for assurance, and your simplicity for allurement. But it's over—This house I no more show my face in.

MISS HARD: I hope, Sir, I have done nothing to disoblige you. I'm sure I should be sorry to affront any gentleman who has been so polite, and said so many civil things to me. I'm sure I should be sorry (*pretending to cry*) if he left the family upon my account. I'm sure I should be sorry, people said any thing amiss, since I have no fortune but my character.

MARL (*Aside*): By heaven, she weeps. This is the first mark of tenderness I ever had from a modest woman, and it touches me. (*To her*) Excuse me, my lovely girl, you are the only part of the family I leave with reluctance. But to be plain with you, the difference of our birth, fortune and education, make an honourable connexion impossible; and I can never harbour a thought of seducing simplicity that trusted in my honour, or bringing ruin upon one, whose only fault was being too lovely.

MISS HARD (*Aside*): Generous man! I now begin to admire him. (*To him*) But I am sure my family is as good as Miss Hardcastle's, and though I'm poor, that's no great misfortune to a contented mind, and, until this moment, I never thought that it was bad to want fortune.

MARL: And why now, my pretty simplicity?

MISS HARD: Because it puts me at a distance from one, that if I had a thousand pound I would give it all to.

MARL (*Aside*): This simplicity bewitches me, so that if I stay I'm undone. I must make one bold effort, and leave her. (*To her*) Your partiality in my favour, my dear, touches me most sensibly, and were I to live for myself alone, I could easily fix my choice. But I owe too much to the opinion of the world, too much to the authority of a father, so that—I can scarcely speak it—it affects me. Farewell.   [Exit

MISS HARD: I never knew half his merit till now. He shall not go, if I have power or art to detain him. I'll still preserve the character in which I stoop'd to conquer but will undeceive my papa, who, perhaps, may laugh him out of his resolution.   [Exit

Enter TONY, MISS NEVILLE

TONY: Ay, you may steal for yourselves the next time. I have done my duty. She has got the jewels again, that's a sure thing; but she believes it was all a mistake of the servants.

MISS NEV: But, my dear cousin, sure you won't forsake us in this distress. If she in the least suspects that I am going off, I shall certainly be locked up, or sent to my aunt Pedigree's, which is ten times worse.

TONY: To be sure, aunts of all kinds are damned bad things. But what can I do? I have got you a pair of horses that will fly like Whistlejacket, and I'm sure you can't say but I have courted you nicely before her face. Here she comes, we must court a bit or two more, for fear she should suspect us.

[They retire, and seem to fondle

Enter MRS. HARDCASTLE

MRS. HARD: Well, I was greatly fluttered, to be sure. But my son tells me it was all a mistake of the servants. I shan't be easy, however, till they are fairly married, and then let her keep her own fortune. But what do I see! Fondling together, as I'm alive. I never saw Tony so sprightly before. Ah! have I caught you, my pretty doves! What, billing, exchanging stolen glances, and broken murmurs. Ah!

TONY: As for murmurs, mother, we grumble a little now and then, to be sure. But there's no love lost between us.

MRS. HARD: A mere sprinkling, Tony, upon the flame, only to make it burn brighter.

MISS NEV: Cousin Tony promises to give us more of his company at home. Indeed, he shan't leave us any more. It won't leave us, cousin Tony, will it?

TONY: O! it's a pretty creature. No, I'd sooner leave my horse in a pound, than leave you when you smile upon one so. Your laugh makes you so becoming.

MISS NEV: Agreeable cousin! Who can help admiring that

natural humour, that pleasant, broad, red, thoughtless (*patting his cheek*) ah! it's a bold face.

MRS. HARD: Pretty innocence!

TONY: I'm sure I always lov'd cousin Con's hazel eyes, and her pretty long fingers, that she twists this way and that, over the haspicolls, like a parcel of bobbins.

MRS. HARD: Ah, he would charm the bird from the tree. I was never so happy before. My boy takes after his father, poor Mr. Lumpkin, exactly. The jewels, my dear Con, shall be yours incontinently. You shall have them. Isn't he a sweet boy, my dear? You shall be married to-morrow, and we'll put off the rest of his education, like Dr. Drowsy's sermons, to a fitter opportunity.

Enter DIGGORY

DIG: Where's the Squire? I have got a letter for your worship.

TONY: Give it to my mamma. She reads all my letters first.

DIG: I had orders to deliver it into your own hands.

TONY: Who does it come from?

DIG: Your worship mun ask that o' the letter itself.

TONY: I could wish to know, though (*turning the letter and gazing on it*).

MISS NEV (*Aside*): Undone, undone! A letter to him from Hastings. I know the hand. If my aunt sees it, we are ruined for ever. I'll keep her employ'd a little if I can. (*To* MRS. HARDCASTLE) But I have not told you, Madam, of my cousin's smart answer just now to Mr. Marlow. We so laugh'd—You must know, Madam—this way a little, for he must not hear us.   [*They confer*

TONY (*Still gazing*): A damn'd cramp piece of penmanship, as ever I saw in my life. I can read your print-hand very well. But here there are such handles, and shanks, and dashes, that one can scarce tell the head from the tail. To Anthony Lumpkin, Esquire. It's very odd, I can read the outside of my letters, where my own name is, well

enough. But when I come to open it, it's all——buzz.
That's hard, very hard; for the inside of the letter is
always the cream of the correspondence.

MRS. HARD: Ha, ha, ha. Very well, very well. And so my
son was too hard for the philosopher.

MISS NEV: Yes, Madam; but you must hear the rest,
Madam. A little more this way, or he may hear us. You'll
hear how he puzzled him again.

MRS. HARD: He seems strangely puzzled now himself,
methinks.

TONY (*Still gazing*): A damn'd up and down hand, as if it
was disguised in liquor. (*Reading*) Dear Sir, Ay, that's
that. Then there's an *M*, and a *T*, and an *S*, but whether
the next be an *izzard*, or an *R*, confound me, I cannot tell.

MRS. HARD: What's that, my dear. Can I gave you any
assistance?

MISS NEV: Pray, aunt, let me read it. Nobody reads a cramp
hand better than I. (*Twitching the letter from him*) Do
you know who it is from?

TONY: Can't tell, except from Dick Ginger the feeder.

MISS NEV: Ay, so it is (*pretending to read*), Dear Squire,
hoping that you're in health, as I am at this present. The
gentlemen of the Shake-bag club has cut the gentlemen of
the Goose-green quite out of feather. The odds——um—
odd battle——um—long fighting—um—here, here, it's
all about cocks, and fighting; it's of no consequence, here,
put it up, put it up.

[*Thrusting the crumpled letter upon him*

TONY: But I tell you, Miss, it's of all the consequence in
the world. I would not lose the rest of it for a guinea.
Here, mother, do you make it out. Of no consequence!

[*Giving* MRS. HARDCASTLE *the letter*

MRS. HARD: How's this! (*reads*) 'Dear Squire, I'm now
waiting for Miss Neville, with a post-chaise and pair, at
the bottom of the garden, but I find my horses yet unable
to perform the journey. I expect you'll assist us with a

pair of fresh horses, as you promised. Dispatch is necessary, as the *hag* (ay, the hag) your mother, will otherwise
suspect us. Yours, Hastings.' Grant me patience. I shall
run distracted. My rage choaks me.

MISS NEV : I hope, Madam, you'll suspend your resentment
for a few moments, and not impute to me any imperti-
nence, or sinister design that belongs to another.

MRS. HARD (*Curtseying very low*): Fine spoken, Madam,
you are most miraculously polite and engaging, and quite
the very pink of courtesy and circumspection, Madam.
(*Changing her tone*) And you, you great ill-fashioned oaf,
with scarce enough sense to keep your mouth shut. Were
you, too, join'd against me? But I'll defeat all your plots
in a moment. As for you, Madam, since you have got a
pair of fresh horses ready, it would be cruel to disappoint
them. So, if you please, instead of running away with
your spark, prepare, this very moment, to run off with
me. Your old aunt Pedigree will keep you secure, I'll
warrant me. You too, Sir, may mount your horse, and
guard us upon the way. Here, Thomas, Roger, Diggory,
I'll shew you, that I wish you better than you do yourselves.   [*Exit*

MISS NEV : So now I'm completely ruined.

TONY : Ay, that's a sure thing.

MISS NEV : What better could be expected from being con-
nected with such a stupid fool, and after all the nods
and signs I made him.

TONY : By the laws, Miss, it was your own cleverness, and
not my stupidity, that did your business. You were so
nice and so busy with your Shake-bags and Goose-greens,
that I thought you could never be making believe.

Enter HASTINGS

HAST : So, Sir, I find by my servant, that you have shewn
my letter, and betray'd us. Was this well done, young
gentleman?

TONY: Here's another. Ask Miss there who betray'd you. Ecod, it was her doing, not mine.

Enter MARLOW

MARL: So I have been finely used here among you. Rendered contemptible, driven into ill manners, despised, insulted, laugh'd at.

TONY: Here's another. We shall have old Bedlam broke loose presently.

MISS NEV: And there, Sir, is the gentleman to whom we all owe every obligation.

MARL: What can I say to him, a mere boy, an ideot, whose ignorance and age are a protection.

HAST: A poor contemptible booby, that would but disgrace correction.

MISS NEV: Yet with cunning and malice enough to make himself merry with all our embarrassments.

HAST: An insensible cub.

MARL: Replete with tricks and mischief.

TONY: Baw! damme, but I'll fight you both one after the other——with baskets.

MARL: As for him, he's below resentment. But your conduct, Mr. Hastings, requires an explanation. You knew of my mistakes, yet would not undeceive me.

HAST: Tortured as I am with my own disappointments, is this a time for explanations? It is not friendly, Mr. Marlow.

MARL: But, Sir——

MISS NEV: Mr. Marlow, we never kept on your mistake, till it was too late to undeceive you. Be pacified.

Enter SERVANT

SERV: My mistress desires you'll get ready immediately, Madam. The horses are putting to. Your hat and things are in the next room. We are to go thirty miles before morning.   [*Exit* SERVANT

MISS NEV: Well, well: I'll come presently.

MARL (*To* HASTINGS): Was it well done, Sir, to assist in rendering me ridiculous. To hang me out for the scorn of all my acquaintance. Depend upon it, Sir, I shall expect an explanation.

HAST: Was it well done, Sir, if you're upon that subject, to deliver what I entrusted to you yourself, to the care of another, Sir.

MISS NEV: Mr. Hastings. Mr. Marlow. Why will you increase my distress by this groundless dispute. I implore, I intreat you——

Enter SERVANT

SERV: Your cloak, Madam. My mistress is impatient.

[*Exit* SERVANT

MISS NEV: I come. Pray be pacified. If I leave you thus, I shall die with apprehension.

Enter SERVANT

SERV: Your fan, muff and gloves, Madam. The horses are waiting.

MISS NEV: O, Mr. Marlow! if you knew what a scene of constraint and ill-nature lies before me, I'm sure it would convert your resentment into pity.

MARL: I'm so distracted with a variety of passions, that I don't know what I do. Forgive me, Madam. George, forgive me. You know my hasty temper, and should not exasperate it.

HAST: The torture of my situation is my only excuse.

MISS NEV: Well, my dear Hastings, if you have that esteem for me that I think, that I am sure you have, your constancy for three years will but increase the happiness of our future connexion. If——

MRS. HARD (*Within*): Miss Neville. Constance, why Constance, I say.

MISS NEV: I'm coming. Well, constancy. Remember, constancy is the word.   [*Exit*

HAST: My heart! How can I support this. To be so near
    happiness, and such happiness.

MARL (*To* TONY): You see now, young gentleman, the
    effects of your folly. What might be amusement to you,
    is here disappointment, and even distress.

TONY (*From a reverie*): Ecod, I have hit it. It's here. Your
    hands. Yours and yours, my poor Sulky. My boots there,
    ho. Meet me two hours hence at the bottom of the garden;
    and if you don't find Tony Lumpkin a more good-natur'd
    fellow than you thought for, I'll give you leave to take
    my best horse, and Bett Bouncer into the bargain. Come
    along. My boots, ho.   [*Exeunt*

ACT V

Enter HASTINGS *and* SERVANT

HAST: You saw the Old Lady and Miss Neville drive off, you say.

SERV: Yes, your honour. They went off in a post-coach, and the young Squire went on horseback. They're thirty miles off by this time.

HAST: Then all my hopes are over.

SERV: Yes, Sir. Old Sir Charles is arrived. He and the Old Gentleman of the house have been laughing at Mr. Marlow's mistake this half hour. They are coming this way.

HAST: Then I must not be seen. So now to my fruitless appointment at the bottom of the garden. This is about the time. [*Exit*

Enter SIR CHARLES *and* HARDCASTLE

HARD: Ha, ha, ha. The peremptory tone in which he sent forth his sublime commands.

SIR CHARL: And the reserve with which I suppose he treated all your advances.

HARD: And yet he might have seen something in me above a common inn-keeper, too.

SIR CHARL: Yes, Dick, but he mistook you for an uncommon inn-keeper, ha, ha, ha.

HARD: Well, I'm in too good spirits to think of any thing but joy. Yes, my dear friend, this union of our families will make our personal friendships hereditary, and tho' my daughter's fortune is but small——

SIR CHARL: Why, Dick, will you talk of fortune to *me*? My son is possessed of more than a competence already, and

can want nothing but a good and virtuous girl to share
his happiness and increase it. If they like each other, as
you say they do——

HARD: *If*, man. I tell you they *do* like each other. My
daughter as good as told me so.

SIR CHARL: But girls are apt to flatter themselves, you
know.

HARD: I saw him grasp her hand in the warmest manner
myself; and here he comes to put you out of your *ifs*, I
warrant him.

Enter MARLOW

MARL: I come, Sir, once more, to ask pardon for my strange
conduct. I can scarce reflect on my insolence without
confusion.

HARD: Tut, boy, a trifle. You take it too gravely. An hour
or two's laughing with my daughter will set all to rights
again. She'll never like you the worse for it.

MARL: Sir, I shall always be proud of her approbation.

HARD: Approbation is but a cold word, Mr. Marlow; if I
am not deceived, you have something more than approbation thereabouts. You take me.

MARL: Really, Sir, I have not that happiness.

HARD: Come, boy, I'm an old fellow, and know what's
what, as well as you that are younger. I know what has
past between you; but mum.

MARL: Sure, Sir, nothing has past between us but the most
profound respect on my side, and the most distant reserve
on hers. You don't think, Sir, that my impudence has
been past upon all the rest of the family.

HARD: Impudence! No. I don't say that—not quite impudence—Though girls like to be play'd with, and rumpled
a little too sometimes. But she has told no tales, I assure
you.

MARL: I never gave her the slightest cause.

HARD: Well, well, I like modesty in its place well enough.

But this is over-acting, young gentleman. You *may* be
open. Your father and I will like you the better for
it.

MARL : May I die, Sir, if I ever——

HARD : I tell you, she don't dislike you; and as I'm sure
you like her——

MARL : Dear Sir—I protest, Sir——

HARD : I see no reason why you should not be joined as
fast as the parson can tie you.

MARL : But hear me, Sir——

HARD : Your father approves the match, I admire it, every
moment's delay will be doing mischief, so—

MARL : But why won't you hear me? By all that's just and
true, I never gave Miss Hardcastle the slightest mark of
my attachment, or even the most distant hint to suspect
me of affection. We had but one interview, and that was
formal, modest, and uninteresting.

HARD (*Aside*): This fellow's formal modest impudence is
beyond bearing.

SIR CHARL: And you never grasp'd her hand, or made any
protestations !

MARL : As heaven is my witness, I came down in obedience
to your commands. I saw the lady without emotion, and
parted without reluctance. I hope you'll exact no further
proofs of my duty, nor prevent me from leaving a house
in which I suffer so many mortifications.   [*Exit*

SIR CHARL: I'm astonished at the air of sincerity with
which he parted.

HARD : And I'm astonished at the deliberate intrepidity of
his assurance.

SIR CHARL: I dare pledge my life and honour upon his
truth.

HARD : Here comes my daughter, and I would stake my
happiness upon her veracity.

Enter MISS HARDCASTLE

HARD: Kate, come hither, child. Answer us sincerely and without reserve: has Mr. Marlow made you any professions of love and affection?

MISS HARD: The question is very abrupt, Sir! But since you require unreserved sincerity, I think he has.

HARD (To SIR CHARLES): You see.

SIR CHARL: And pray, Madam, have you and my son had more than one interview?

MISS HARD: Yes, Sir, several.

HARD (To SIR CHARLES): You see.

SIR CHARL: But did he profess any attachment?

MISS HARD: A lasting one.

SIR CHARL: Did he talk of love?

MISS HARD: Much, Sir.

SIR CHARL: Amazing! And all this formally?

MISS HARD: Formally.

HARD: Now, my friend, I hope you are satisfied.

SIR CHARL: And how did he behave, Madam?

MISS HARD: As most profest admirers do. Said some civil things of my face, talked much of his want of merit, and the greatness of mine; mentioned his heart, gave a short tragedy speech, and ended with pretended rapture.

SIR CHARL: Now I'm perfectly convinced, indeed. I know his conversation among women to be modest and submissive. This forward canting ranting manner by no means describes him, and I am confident he never sate for the picture.

MISS HARD: Then what, Sir, if I should convince you to your face of my sincerity? if you and my papa, in about half an hour, will place yourselves behind that screen, you shall hear him declare his passion to me in person.

SIR CHARL: Agreed. And if I find him what you describe, all my happiness in him must have an end. [Exit

MISS HARD: And if you don't find him what I describe——
I fear my happiness must never have a beginning.

[Exeunt

SCENE CHANGES TO THE BACK OF THE
GARDEN

Enter HASTINGS

HAST: What an ideot am I, to wait here for a fellow, who
probably takes a delight in mortifying me. He never
intended to be punctual, and I'll wait no longer. What
do I see! It is he! and perhaps with news of my
Constance.

Enter TONY, *booted and spattered*

HAST: My honest Squire! I now find you a man of your
word. This looks like friendship.

TONY: Ay, I'm your friend, and the best friend you have
in the world, if you knew but all. This riding by night,
by the bye, is cursedly tiresome. It has shook me worse
than the basket of a stage-coach.

HAST: But how? where did you leave your fellow travellers?
Are they in safety? Are they housed?

TONY: Five and twenty miles in two hours and a half is no
such bad driving. The poor beasts have smoaked for it:
Rabbet me, but I'd rather ride forty miles after a fox than
ten with such *varment*.

HAST: Well, but where have you left the ladies? I die with
impatience.

TONY: Left them! Why where should I leave them, but
where I found them.

HAST: This is a riddle.

TONY: Riddle me this then. What's that goes round the
house, and round the house, and never touches the
house?

HAST: I'm still astray.

TONY: Why, that's it, mon. I have led them astray. By
jingo, there's not a pond or a slough within five miles of
the place but they can tell the taste of.

HAST: Ha, ha, ha, I understand; you took them in a round,

while they supposed themselves going forward, and so
you have at last brought them home again.

TONY: You shall hear. I first took them down Feather-
bed-lane, where we stuck fast in the mud. I then rattled
them crack over the stones of Up-and-down Hill—I
then introduced them to the gibbet on Heavy-tree
Heath, and from that, with a circumbendibus, I fairly
lodged them in the horse-pond at the bottom of the
garden.

HAST: But no accident, I hope.

TONY: No, no. Only mother is confoundedly frightened.
She thinks herself forty miles off. She's sick of the
journey, and the cattle can scarce crawl. So if your own
horses be ready, you may whip off with cousin, and I'll
be bound that no soul here can budge a foot to follow
you.

HAST: My dear friend, how can I be grateful!

TONY: Ay, now it's dear friend, noble Squire. Just now, it
was all ideot, cub, and run me through the guts. Damn
your way of fighting, I say. After we take a knock in
this part of the country, we kiss and be friends. But if
you had run me through the guts, then I should be dead,
and you might go kiss the hangman.

HAST: The rebuke is just. But I must hasten to relieve Miss
Neville; if you keep the old lady employed, I promise to
take care of the young one.   [Exit HASTINGS

TONY: Never fear me. Here she comes. Vanish. She's got
from the pond, and draggled up to the waist like a
mermaid.

Enter MRS. HARDCASTLE

MRS. HARD: Oh, Tony, I'm killed. Shook. Battered to death.
I shall never survive it. That last jolt that laid us against
the quickset hedge has done my business.

TONY: Alack, Mama, it was all your own fault. You would
be for running away by night, without knowing one inch

of the way.

MRS. HARD: I wish we were at home again. I never met so many accidents in so short a journey. Drench'd in the mud, overturn'd in a ditch, stuck fast in a slough, jolted to a jelly, and at last to lose our way. Whereabouts do you think we are, Tony?

TONY: By my guess we should come upon Crackskull common, about forty miles from home.

MRS. HARD: O lud! O lud! The most notorious spot in all the country. We only want a robbery to make a complete night on 't.

TONY: Don't be afraid, Mama, don't be afraid. Two of the five that kept here are hanged, and the other three may not find us. Don't be afraid. Is that a man that's galloping behind us? No; it's only a tree. Don't be afraid.

MRS. HARD: The fright will certainly kill me.

TONY: Do you see any thing like a black hat moving behind the thicket?

MRS. HARD: O death!

TONY: No, it's only a cow. Don't be afraid, Mama; don't be afraid.

MRS. HARD: As I'm alive, Tony, I see a man coming towards us. Ah! I'm sure on 't. If he perceives us we are undone.

TONY (Aside): Father-in-law, by all that's unlucky, come to take one of his night walks. (To her) Ah, it's a highwayman, with pistols as long as my arm. A damn'd ill-looking fellow.

MRS. HARD: Good Heaven defend us? He approaches.

TONY: Do you hide yourself in that thicket, and leave me to manage him. If there be any danger I'll cough and cry hem. When I cough be sure to keep close.

[MRS. HARDCASTLE *hides behind a tree in the back scene*

Enter HARDCASTLE

HARD: I'm mistaken, or I heard voices of people in want of

help. Oh, Tony, is that you? I did not expect you so soon back. Are your mother and her charge in safety?

TONY: Very safe, Sir, at my aunt Pedigree's. Hem.

MRS. HARD (*From behind*): Ah death! I find there's danger.

HARD: Forty miles in three hours; sure, that's too much, my youngster.

TONY: Stout horses and willing minds make short journeys, as they say. Hem.

MRS. HARD (*From behind*): Sure he'll do the dear boy no harm.

HARD: But I heard a voice here; I should be glad to know from whence it came.

TONY: It was I, Sir, talking to myself, Sir. I was saying that forty miles in four hours was very good going. Hem. As to be sure it was. Hem. I have got a sort of cold by being out in the air. We'll go in, if you please. Hem.

HARD: But if you talk'd to yourself, you did not answer yourself. I'm certain I heard two voices, and am resolved (*raising his voice*) to find the other out.

MRS. HARD (*From behind*): Oh! he's coming to find me out. Oh!

TONY: What need you go, Sir, if I tell you. Hem. I'll lay down my life for the truth—hem—I'll tell you all, Sir.

[*Detaining him*

HARD: I tell you, I will not be detained. I insist on seeing. It's in vain to expect I'll believe you.

MRS. HARD (*Running forward from behind*): O lud, he'll murder my poor boy, my darling. Here, good gentleman, whet your rage upon me. Take my money, my life, but spare that young gentleman, spare my child, if you have any mercy.

HARD: My wife! as I'm a Christian. From whence can she come, or what does she mean!

MRS. HARD (*Kneeling*): Take compassion on us, good Mr.

Highwayman. Take our money, our watches, all we have, but spare our lives. We will never bring you to justice, indeed we won't, good Mr. Highwayman.

HARD: I believe the woman's out of her senses. What, Dorothy, don't you know me?

MRS. HARD: Mr. Hardcastle, as I'm alive! My fears blinded me. But who, my dear, could have expected to meet you here, in this frightful place, so far from home. What has brought you to follow us?

HARD: Sure, Dorothy, you have not lost your wits. So far from home, when you are within forty yards of your own door. (To him) This is one of your old tricks, you graceless rogue you. (To her) Don't you know the gate, and the mulberry tree; and don't you remember the horse-pond, my dear?

MRS. HARD: Yes, I shall remember the horse-pond as long as I live; I have caught my death in it. (To TONY) And is it to you, you graceless varlet, I owe all this? I'll teach you to abuse your mother, I will.

TONY: Ecod, Mother, all the parish says you have spoil'd me, and so you may take the fruits on 't.

MRS. HARD: I'll spoil you, I will.

[Follows him off the stage. Exit

HARD: There's morality, however, in his reply.   [Exit

Enter HASTINGS and MISS NEVILLE

HAST: My dear Constance, why will you deliberate thus? If we delay a moment, all is lost for ever. Pluck up a little resolution, and we shall soon be out of the reach of her malignity.

MISS NEV: I find it impossible. My spirits are so sunk with the agitations I have suffered, that I am unable to face any new danger. Two or three years patience will at last crown us with happiness.

HAST: Such a tedious delay is worse than inconstancy. Let us fly, my charmer. Let us date our happiness from this

very moment. Perish fortune. Love and content will
increase what we possess beyond a monarch's revenue.
Let me prevail.

MISS NEV: No, Mr. Hastings; no. Prudence once more
comes to my relief, and I will obey its dictates. In the
moment of passion, fortune may be despised, but it ever
produces a lasting repentance. I'm resolved to apply to
Mr. Hardcastle's compassion and justice for redress.

HAST: But though he had the will, he has not the power to
relieve you.

MISS NEV: But he has influence and upon that I am
resolved to rely.

HAST: I have no hopes. But since you persist, I must reluctantly obey you.   [*Exeunt*

SCENE CHANGES

Enter SIR CHARLES *and* MISS HARDCASTLE

SIR CHARL: What a situation am I in. If what you say
appears, I shall then find a guilty son. If what he says be
true, I shall then lose one that, of all others, I most wish'd
for a daughter.

MISS HARD: I am proud of your approbation, and to shew
I merit it, if you place yourselves as I directed, you shall
hear his explicit declaration. But he comes.

SIR CHARL: I'll to your father, and keep him to the appointment.   [*Exit* SIR CHARLES

Enter MARLOW

MARL: Tho' prepared for setting out, I come once more to
take leave, nor did I, till this moment, know the pain I
feel in the separation.

MISS HARD (*In her own natural manner*): I believe these
sufferings cannot be very great, Sir, which you can so
easily remove. A day or two longer, perhaps, might
lessen your uneasiness, by shewing the little value of
what you now think proper to regret.

MARL (*Aside*): This girl every moment improves upon me. (*To her*) It must not be, Madam. I have already trifled too long with my heart. My very pride begins to submit to my passion. The disparity of education and fortune, the anger of a parent, and the contempt of my equals, begin to lose their weight; and nothing can restore me to myself, but this painful effort of resolution.

MISS HARD: Then go, Sir. I'll urge nothing more to detain you. Though my family be as good as hers you came down to visit, and my education, I hope, not inferior, what are these advantages without equal affluence? I must remain contented with the slight approbation of imputed merit; I must have only the mockery of your addresses, while all your serious aims are fixed on fortune.

Enter HARDCASTLE *and* SIR CHARLES *from behind*

SIR CHARL: Here, behind this screen.

HARD: Ay, ay, make no noise. I'll engage my Kate covers him with confusion at last.

MARL: By heavens, Madam, fortune was ever my smallest consideration. Your beauty at first caught my eye; for who could see that without emotion. But every moment that I converse with you, steals in some new grace, heightens the picture, and gives it stronger expression. What at first seem'd rustic plainness, now appears refin'd simplicity. What seem'd forward assurance, now strikes me as the result of courageous innocence, and conscious virtue.

SIR CHARL: What can it mean! He amazes me!

HARD: I told you how it would be. Hush!

MARL: I am now determined to stay, Madam, and I have too good an opinion of my father's discernment, when he sees you, to doubt his approbation.

MISS HARD: No, Mr. Marlow, I will not, cannot detain you. Do you think I could suffer a connexion, in which there is the smallest room for repentance? Do you think I would take the mean advantage of a transient passion, to load you with confusion? Do you think I could ever relish that happiness, which was acquired by lessening yours?

MARL: By all that's good, I can have no happiness but what's in your power to grant me. Nor shall I ever feel repentance, but in not having seen your merits before. I will stay, even contrary to your wishes; and tho' you should persist to shun me, I will make my respectful assiduities atone for the levity of my past conduct.

MISS HARD: Sir, I must entreat you'll desist. As our acquaintance began, so let it end, in indifference. I might have given an hour or two to levity; but seriously, Mr. Marlow, do you think I could ever submit to a connexion, where I must appear mercenary and *you* imprudent? Do you think I could ever catch at the confident addresses of a secure admirer?

MARL (*Kneeling*): Does this look like security? Does this look like confidence? No, Madam, every moment that shews me your merit, only serves to increase my diffidence and confusion. Here let me continue——

SIR CHARL: I can hold it no longer. Charles, Charles, how hast thou deceived me! Is this your indifference, your uninteresting conversation?

HARD: Your cold contempt; your formal interview. What have you to say now?

MARL: That I'm all amazement. What can it mean!

HARD: It means that you can say and unsay things at pleasure. That you can address a lady in private, and deny it in public; that you have one story for us, and another for my daughter!

MARL: Daughter!—This lady your daughter!

HARD: Yes, Sir, my only daughter. My Kate, whose else should she be?

MARL: Oh, the devil.

MISS HARD: Yes, Sir, that very identical tall squinting lady you were pleased to take me for (*curtseying*). She that you addressed as the mild, modest, sentimental man of gravity, and the bold forward agreeable rattle of the ladies club, ha, ha, ha.

MARL: Zounds, there's no bearing this; it's worse than death.

MISS HARD: In which of your characters, Sir, will you give us leave to address you? As the faultering gentleman, with looks on the ground, that speaks just to be heard, and hates hypocrisy; or the loud confident creature, that keeps it up with Mrs. Mantrap, and old Miss Biddy Buckskin, till three in the morning; ha, ha, ha.

MARL: O, curse on my noisy head. I never attempted to be impudent yet, that I was not taken down. I must be gone.

HARD: By the hand of my body, but you shall not. I see it was all a mistake, and I am rejoiced to find it. You shall not, Sir, I tell you. I know she'll forgive you. Won't you forgive him, Kate. We'll all forgive you. Take courage, man. [*They retire, she tormenting him, to the back scene*

Enter MRS. HARDCASTLE, TONY

MRS. HARD: So, so, they're gone off. Let them go, I care not.

HARD: Who gone?

MRS. HARD: My dutiful niece and her gentleman, Mr. Hastings, from Town. He who came down with our modest visitor here.

SIR CHARL: Who, my honest George Hastings? As worthy a fellow as lives, and the girl could not have made a more prudent choice.

HARD: Then, by the hand of my body, I'm proud of the connexion.

MRS. HARD: Well, if he has taken away the lady, he has not taken her fortune; that remains in this family to console us for her loss.

HARD: Sure, Dorothy, you would not be so mercenary?

MRS. HARD: Ay, that's my affair, not yours.

HARD: But you know if your son, when of age, refuses to marry his cousin, her whole fortune is then at her own disposal.

MRS. HARD: Ay, but he's not of age, and she has not thought proper to wait for his refusal.

Enter HASTINGS *and* MISS NEVILLE

MRS. HARD: (*Aside*): What, returned so soon! I begin not to like it.

HAST (*To* HARDCASTLE): For my late attempt to fly off with your niece, let my present confusion be my punishment. We are now come back, to appeal from your justice to your humanity. By her father's consent, I first paid her my addresses, and our passions were first founded in duty.

MISS NEV: Since his death, I have been obliged to stoop to dissimulation to avoid oppression. In an hour of levity, I was ready even to give up my fortune to secure my choice. But I'm now recover'd from the delusion, and hope from your tenderness what is denied me from a nearer connexion.

MRS. HARD: Pshaw, pshaw, this is all but the whining end of a modern novel.

HARD: Be it what it will, I'm glad they're come back to reclaim their due. Come hither, Tony boy. Do you refuse this lady's hand whom I now offer you?

TONY: What signifies my refusing. You know I can't refuse her till I'm of age, Father.

HARD: While I thought concealing your age, boy, was likely to conduce to your improvement, I concurred with your mother's desire to keep it secret. But since I find she turns it to a wrong use, I must now declare you have been of age these three months.

TONY: Of age! Am I of age, Father?

HARD: Above three months.

TONY: Then you'll see the first use I'll make of my liberty. (*Taking* MISS NEVILLE'S *hand*) Witness all men by these presents, that I Anthony Lumpkin, Esquire, of BLANK place, refuse you, Constantia Neville, spinster, of no place at all, for my true and lawful wife. So Constance Neville may marry whom she pleases, and Tony Lumpkin is his own man again.

SIR CHARL: O brave Squire.

HAST: My worthy friend!

MRS. HARD: My undutiful offspring!

MARL: Joy, my dear George, I give you joy sincerely. And could I prevail upon my little tyrant here to be less arbitrary, I should be the happiest man alive, if you would return me the favour.

HAST (*To* MISS HARDCASTLE): Come, Madam, you are now driven to the very last scene of all your contrivances. I know you like him, I'm sure he loves you, and you must and shall have him.

HARD (*Joining their hands*): And I say so too. And, Mr. Marlow, if she makes as good a wife as she has a daughter, I don't believe you'll ever repent your bargain. So now to supper. To-morrow we shall gather all the poor of the parish about us, and the Mistakes of the Night shall be crown'd with a merry morning; so, boy, take her, and as you have been mistaken in the mistress, my wish is, that you may never be mistaken in the wife.

[*Exeunt omnes*

77

EPILOGUE

BY DR. GOLDSMITH

SPOKEN BY MRS. BULKLEY

in the Character of

MISS HARDCASTLE

Well, having stoop'd to conquer with success,
And gain'd a husband without aid from dress,
Still, as a barmaid, I could wish it too,
As I have conquer'd him, to conquer you:
And let me say, for all your resolution,
That pretty barmaids have done execution.
Our life is all a play, compos'd to please,
'We have our exits and our entrances.'
The first act shows the simple country maid,
Harmless and young, of ev'ry thing afraid;
Blushes when hir'd, and with unmeaning action,
I hopes as how to give you satisfaction.
Her second act displays a livelier scene—
Th' unblushing barmaid of a country inn,
Who whisks about the house, at market caters,
Talks loud, coquets the guests, and scolds the waiters.
Next the scene shifts to town, and there she soars,
The chop-house toast of ogling connoisseurs.
On Squires and Cits she there displays her arts,
And on the gridiron broils her lovers' hearts—
And as she smiles, her triumphs to compleat,
E'en Common Councilmen forget to eat.
The fourth act shows her wedded to the Squire,
And Madam now begins to hold it higher;
Pretends to taste, at Operas cries caro,

And quits her Nancy Dawson, for Che Faro:
Doats upon dancing, and in all her pride
Swims round the room, the Heinel of Cheapside:
Ogles and leers with artificial skill,
Till having lost in age the power to kill,
She sits all night at cards, and ogles at spadille.
Such, thro' our lives the eventful history—
The fifth and last act still remains for me.
The barmaid now for your protection prays,
Turns Female Barrister, and pleads for Bayes.

EPILOGUE[1]

To be Spoken in the Character of

TONY LUMPKIN

BY J. CRADOCK, ESQ.

Well—now all's ended—and my comrades gone,
Pray what becomes of mother's nonly son?
A hopeful blade!—in town I'll fix my station,
And try to make a bluster in the nation;
As for my cousin Neville, I renounce her,
Off—in a crack—I'll carry big Bett Bouncer.
  Why should not I in the great world appear?
I soon shall have a thousand pounds a year;
No matter what a man may here inherit,
In London—'gad, they've some regard to spirit.
I see the horses prancing up the streets,
And big Bett Bouncer bobs to all she meets;
Then hoikes to jigs and pastimes ev'ry night—
Not to the plays—they say it a'n't polite;
To Sadler's Wells perhaps, or Operas go,
And once, by chance, to the roratorio.
Thus here and there, for ever up and down,
We'll set the fashions too, to half the town;
And then at auctions—money ne'er regard,
Buy pictures like the great, ten pounds a yard;
Zounds, we shall make these London gentry say,
We know what's damn'd genteel, as well as they.

[1] This came too late to be spoken.

Notes

The notes in this edition are intended to serve the needs of overseas students as well as those of British-born users.

Inverted commas indicates references to stage directions.

Dedication

xxvii *Samuel Johnson*: Dr Johnson (1709–84) was a friend of Goldsmith, and one of the most important literary figures of the eighteenth century. He is best remembered today for his compilation of his dictionary, and is immortalized in his biography by James Boswell.

   the greatest wit ... unaffected piety: his sharp wit which did not prevent Johnson from being a religious man.

   your partiality...: Johnson had persuaded George Colman (1732–94), the manager of the Covent Garden Theatre, to produce *She Stoops to Conquer*. This had not been easy, and two of the actors had refused to take part in it. When Goldsmith took the play to David Garrick (1717–79) at the Drury Lane Theatre, Colman, anxious that his rival might make the play a success, reluctantly agreed to stage it.

   a Comedy, not merely sentimental: Colman's main worry was that the play represented a reaction to the highly popular sentimental comedies of the time.

   late in the season: the play appeared in March, and the season ended on 31 May. When holidays and actors' benefit nights were accounted for, this left a mere dozen occasions on which the play could be performed.

Prologue

xxviii *David Garrick*: perhaps the most famous of all English actors. He was also manager of the Drury Lane Theatre, and wrote several minor plays, and various prologues and epilogues to other writers' plays, as is the case here.

'MR WOODWARD': Henry Woodward (1717–77) was an actor who specialized in comic parts. He played Lofty in Goldsmith's *The Good Natur'd Man* (1768), and was due to play Tony Lumpkin but turned down the part. However, he agreed to speak the Prologue.

'Tis not alone this mourning suit ... I've that within: compare Hamlet's words in Shakespeare's play ''Tis not alone my inky cloak, good mother... That can denote me truly...' (I.ii. 77–86).

The Comic muse: in Greek mythology there were nine muses, who were the daughters of Zeus and Mnemosyne. Thalia was the muse of comedy and pastoral poetry.

play'r: player, actor.

sweet maid: Thalia, the 'Comic muse.'

Shuter: Edward (Ned) Shuter (1728–76) was a comic actor who played the part of Hardcastle. He had previously played Croaker in *The Good Natur'd Man*.

mawkish drab: a feebly sentimental female of low taste and character.

sentimentals ... sentiments: referring to the play's attack on the popular sentimental comedy, whose typical tone of pious and obvious moralizing is parodied further on in the Prologue ('All is not gold that glitters ... virtue is not virtue, if she tumble').

be moral: again, referring to the moralizing manner of sentimental comedy.

My heart thus pressing ... sententious look: presumably at this point the actor places his hand over his heart and sets his face in a way that affects emotion.

blocks: wooden heads with no features, used for moulding hats or as wig-stands – that is, they show no genuine feeling.

All is not gold that glitters: an English proverb which was old when Shakespeare used it in *The Merchant of Venice*, and typical of the commonplace maxims that follow.

xxix _*tumble:* probably with a secondary sexual meaning.

morals: moral maxims.

To make you laugh I must play tragedy: that is, he would be a failure as a sentimental actor, and so if no comedies were written then he would be forced to act in tragedies; and he would be so bad in those that the audience would laugh at him.

the maid: the 'Comic muse'.

A doctor: Goldsmith held a Bachelor of Medicine degree, and is here conceived as tending to the sick muse of Comedy.

five draughts: five doses; that is, the five acts of the play.

The college you ... regular ... quack: you, the audience, are to judge his competence as a doctor; you are like a college of physicians or surgeons, whose applause will show that he is to be accepted as a 'regular' (that is, properly qualified), or whose disapproval will pronounce him a 'quack' (that is, fraudulent amateur).

Act I

Scene 1

1 *particular:* used here in the sense of peculiar, odd, strange.

to town: to London.

to rub off the rust: that is, to refresh or recreate oneself.

Miss Hoggs ... Mrs Grigsby: The names suggest minor country people. Hogg calls to mind a pig, and a grig is a small person or animal.

fopperies: silly affectations, foolish vanities.

basket: the outside baggage-container of a stagecoach, which was also used as a seat by the poorer passengers. Hence, Mr Hardcastle is saying that the follies of the upper classes (who would have been inside passengers) have spread to other classes in the country districts.

rumbling: an old-fashioned usage for rambling.

Oddfish ... Cripplegate: again, the names are deliberately debasing, almost as if to underline Mrs Hardcastle's attitude towards them ('gate' = 'gait', or way of walking). It is ironic that all the country can boast in the way of a dancing-master is a lame one.

Prince Eugene and the Duke of Marlborough: Prince Eugene of Savoy (1663–1736) led the forces of the Emperor Leopold I in the War of the Spanish Succession, and was an ally of John Churchill, Duke of Marlborough (1650–1722) at the Battle of Blenheim (1704), in which the French were defeated.

trumpery: worthless trifles.

2 *Darby ... Joan:* a ballad was composed in the eighteenth century celebrating the devotion for each other of John Darby and his wife Joan. The names have become proverbial for a happy old couple.

make money of that: an obsolete saying, which means 'see if you can make anything out of that'. She is here challenging her husband to make her age more than forty, but he teases her by suggesting that a truer addition of her sum would be fifty-seven. Assuming her memory to be correct as to her age when Tony was born, and given the fact that we are soon to learn that Tony is not yet twenty-one, then we must conclude that Hardcastle is joking, and that she is nearer to her figure than his.

years of discretion: twenty-one, traditionally the age at which a young person in England 'comes of age', and becomes legally responsible for all his own actions, and entitled to dispose of any money that he may have inherited. Not long ago the age was lowered, in most respects, to eighteen.

quotha!: 'says you!' An expression of contemptuous disbelief.

Humour ... humour ... humour: the word is used here in its former sense of a particular physical condition which determines temperament and character. There were supposed to be four *humours* or fluids in the body: the *sanguine*, which was believed to be indicated by a red face and optimistic outlook or boisterous habits; the *choleric*, marked by high blood-pressure and explosive temper; the *phlegmatic*, stolid and imperturbable; the *melancholic*, sad and depressed. The characteristic temperament of the English is commonly believed to be phlegmatic, but Tony Lumpkin was evidently of the sanguine type.

allow him an horse-pond: throw him into a horse-pond. Troublesome or unpopular persons were sometimes pitched into a horse-pond as an informal and unceremonious punishment.

frighting: frightening.

fastened my wig to the back of my chair: Lord Nugent records: 'One evening at Gosfield, she [Lord Clare's daughter] tied the tail of his [Goldsmith's] wig, whilst he was asleep, to the back of his chair. When he woke, and his wig came off, he, knowing at once who was the practical joker of the family, threatened to revenge himself upon her. He was then writing *She Stoops to Conquer*, and his revenge was to make Tony Lumpkin the hero in precisely the same trick.'

sickly: in poor health. This is one of Mrs Hardcastle's motherly illusions about her son, who is in fact robust and healthy.

cat and fiddle: a familiar proverbial expression which suggested an unlikely combination. Mr Hardcastle means 'Nonsense!' As the cat and the fiddle is also often used as a tavern sign, he may also have had in mind that Tony Lumpkin is more familiar with alehouses than with Latin. All English children will have come across the English nursery rhyme which begins, 'Hey diddle, diddle, the cat and the fiddle...'.

3 *snub:* reprimand, humiliatingly rebuke.

speaking trumpet: conical-shaped instrument for magnifying the voice.

Papa and I: grammatically incorrect for 'Papa and me'.

The Three Pigeons: the name of the local tavern. After the play appeared, the local inn at Lissoy, the village in Ireland where Goldsmith grew up, was called by this name.

exciseman: a customs man whose job was to collect duty on imported goods and prevent smuggling.

horse doctor: veterinary surgeon.

Aminadab: slang term for a Quaker.

music box: barrel-organ, hurdy-gurdy or similar mechanical instrument.

spins the pewter platter: spins plates on the end of a stick. Note that Tony's boon companions were a motley assortment, and seem to have included fairground and street-corner entertainers. As often in this play, the names are significant, and here indicate that their owners are extremely 'low' (e.g. a muggins is a fool, and 'slang' means 'nonsense' or 'humbug').

4 *'Solus':* (Latin) alone.

gauze: a fine, transparent material.

frippery: cheap finery.

the indigent world: all the poor and needy people.

housewife's dress: her wearing of this plain form of dress later in the play helps to lead to Marlow's thinking her the barmaid.

5 *pitched:* fixed, settled.

mortify: humiliate, upset.

break my glass for its flattery: her mirror shows her that her face is very attractive; hence, if any young man can resist her good looks then it seems that the mirror must have been flattering her, and thus it deserves to be broken.

my cap: young women of the age usually wore indoors a light cap trimmed with lace or ribbons.

6 *recruits ... muster:* they are like untrained recruits at their first parade – that is, very disorganized.

Lud: a polite form of 'Lord!'

sheepish: shy and awkward in company.

whimsical: odd-looking.

in face: looking attractive.

no accident has happened ... too moving: through Miss Neville's words, Goldsmith is here mocking the appropriate 'sentimental' response to Kate's news.

7 *of another stamp:* that is, of a lower class.

tête-à-têtes: intimate and confidential discussions between two persons (from the French meaning, literally, 'head-to-head').

setting off her pretty monster: giving a flattering account of her son, Tony.

pink: highest, ultimate. The expression 'in the pink', meaning 'going along splendidly', is still used.

be too hard for her at last: outmanoeuvre her in the end.

improvements: referring to the current fashion for 'improving' houses and landscaping gardens.

Allons: (French) Let's go.

Would it were bedtime and all were well: Kate is quoting Falstaff's words on the day of the battle of Shrewbury in Shakespeare's *Henry IV, Part 1* (see V.i. 125–6).

'Exeunt': (Latin) plural of 'exit', and meaning 'they go out'.

Scene 2

8 *'punch':* wine or other alcoholic drink mixed with spices and fruit, and then heated.

'OMNES': (Latin) all.

Hurrea: hurrah.

knock himself down for a song: Tony is acting as chairman and master of ceremonies, and as such he will hammer on the table with his mallet and announce that he will sing. There is probably an unkind pun on the auctioneering term 'to knock down for a song', implying to sell cheaply.

genus: probably a pun meaning (1) mankind (Latin), (2) genius (it could be a dialect pronunciation).

Lethes ... Styxes: Lethe and Styx were rivers of the underworld in classical mythology.

Stygians: as gloomy as the river Styx.

Quis ... Quaes ... Quods: relative pronouns in Latin meaning their 'whos' and their 'whiches' and their 'whats'. Every schoolboy would have learned these by heart, and by pluralizing them here Tony is showing his contempt for all 'learning'.

Pigeons: slang for fools who are easily cheated.

Toroddle, toroddle, toroll: a meaningless chorus, to be sung by all as noisily as possible.

Methodist preachers: Methodism was founded by Charles Wesley (1707–88) as a reaction against the laxity which he saw in many in the Church of England. Travelling preachers went out all over the country, and their open-air meetings and emotional oratory had a powerful effect. The most famous preachers were John Wesley (1703–91), brother to Charles, and George Whitefield (1714–70). Methodists were rigidly opposed to alcoholic drinks.

crown: silver five-shilling piece (modern equivalent 25 p).

skinful: bellyful of strong liquor.

jorum: punch-bowl.

9 *bustards:* a species of large game bird.

widgeons: a species of wild duck.

spunk: spirit.

bekeays: countryman's pronunciation of 'because'.

low: common; disreputable.

bees: is (country dialect).

concatenation: an uninterrupted chain of events or thoughts. However, the speaker is here merely trying to impress by using a fine-sounding word without knowing what it means. Goldsmith is incidentally mocking the niceties of speech employed by the bourgeois audience who had considered *The Good Natur'd Man* to be 'low'.

maxum: maxim (again, country dialect). The yokels are being 'sentimental', in the sense that they are enjoying the kind of pious sentiment which was typical of plays of the period.

obligated to dance a bear: he earns his living by leading about a dancing bear and thereby begging money from on-lookers.

Water Parted: a song from *Artaxerxes* (1762), an opera by Thomas Arne (1710–78). He was the most popular composer of the period, and is best remembered today for the tune of 'Rule Britannia!'

Ariadne: an opera (1734) by George Handel (1685–1759), the German composer who spent much of his life in London, where he became Court Musician to George I. His choral work, *The Messiah*, is his greatest achievement. He was an outstanding composer of the eighteenth century.

come to his own: old enough to inherit and use the money left to him by his father.

Ecod: By God.

winding the straight horn: blowing a hunting horn.

be no bastard: show by my behaviour that I'm the true son of my father.

pay no reckoning: don't have to pay the bill.

Stingo: a strong ale or beer, here used as a slang word for the landlord of a tavern.

10 *post-chaise:* a hired horse-drawn carriage. Up to four people could travel inside, with the driver sitting on one of the horses.

upo': upon, in.

woundily: extremely ('woundily' being an adaption of the oath 'by God's wounds').

in the squeezing of a lemon: that is, in less time than it takes to squeeze a lemon.

Father-in-law: this term is now confined to the father of a person's wife or husband; we would now refer to Mr Hardcastle as Tony's stepfather.

whelp: young dog; applied here in the sense of ill-behaved youth.

grumbletonian: grumbler. Originally the word was used as a nickname for the country party, as opposed to the Court party, in the reign of William and Mary. The name arose probably because country dwellers were accustomed to grumble when they compared their condition with the prosperity of those surrounding the Court in London.

threescore: sixty (3 × 20).

unaccountable reserve: Marlow's strange character is quickly emphasized.

unmannerly: impolite, rude.

11 *wanted no ghost:* Marlow is echoing Shakespeare's *Hamlet* (I.v. 128).

cross-grain'd: bad-tempered.

trapesing: lolloping, ungainly.

trolloping: untidy, slovenly.

maypole: slang term for a tall and thin person.

awkward: former spelling of 'awkward'.

mother's apron-string: proverbial for a child being tied to the influence of its mother.

Lock-a-daisy: lack-a-daisy, from 'alack-a-day', meaning 'alas'.

12 *Squash-lane:* presumably a very boggy road, as 'squash' meant 'splash'.

Crack-skull Common … Murrain's: the countryside is made to sound as dangerous and uninviting as possible. Country lanes would have had no metalled surface and been deeply rutted with wheel-tracks which could easily break a horse's leg. Crack-skull suggests a place of violent robbery, and a murrain was a plague.

Zounds: an abbreviated form of the oath 'by God's wounds'.

longitude: in 1713 a prize of £20,000 was offered to anybody who could devise a way of accurately calculating longitude at sea. An English clockmaker called John Harrison

(1693–1776) eventually made one which, when tested on a long voyage in 1762, was found to have lost less than two minutes. After the intervention of King George III on Harrison's behalf, the government grudgingly paid him the maximum prize in 1773, three months after this play opened.

13 *ben't:* be not (country dialect) = are not.

sending them to your father's as an inn: a trick of this kind was played on Goldsmith himself when he was young.

Mum: not a word!

his mother ... justice of peace: as at that time women could not hold offices of this kind, Tony is saying that Mr Hardcastle will make ridiculous boasts about his relatives.

blade: dashing, hearty character. 'Blade' originally meant that a man of such a temperament would have worn a sword.

a': he

connexion: (connection) relationship, communication (with him).

Act II

14 *side-table:* one to which cooked dishes are carried from the kitchen and thence served to the guests at the dining-table.

blockhead: one who behaves so stupidly that one would think his head to be made of wood.

militia: a non-professional branch of the British army who acted as a national auxiliary reserve, or 'home' guard; the forerunner of the modern volunteer Territorial Army.

parfectly unpossible ... yeating: country dialect for 'perfectly impossible ... eating'. It is not clear whether all the dialect words which Goldsmith employs were actually in usage, or whether he is deliberately exaggerating the country dialect for comic effect.

15 *Stay your stomach:* satisfy your hunger.

We have laughed at that these twenty years: it is not clear whether the simple country servants have found the same story genuinely amusing over and over again, or whether this is Diggory's sly way of indicating that Hardcastle's best story is a very stale one.

bauld: (dialect) bold.

pleace: (dialect) place.

sartain: (dialect) certain.

Wauns: dialect corruption of 'Zounds' (see note to page 12 above).

canna: (dialect) cannot.

numskulls: stupid people with skulls too thick to sense anything.

quarrelling for places: referring to the scramble for government positions (places) by contemporary politicians.

16 *elevens:* perhaps 'heavens', or possibly a reference to the eleven apostles (minus Judas, who betrayed Jesus).

Ize: (dialect) I'll.

good housekeeping: lavish spending on household goods and hospitality; this is an ironic pun, since the phrase normally means careful spending on household necessities.

levy contributions: earn money.

inflame a reckoning: increase the bill. This echoes a phrase in *The Two Noble Kinsman* (published 1634) by John Fletcher (1579–1625), probably in collaboration with Shakespeare. See III.v. 130.

confoundedly: exceedingly.

The Englishman's malady: that is, a reserved and shy nature.

that lovely part of the creation: that is, women.

17 *of all conscience:* indeed.

ideot: idiot.

Faith: abbreviated form of the oath 'in faith', meaning 'believe me'.

rattle away: chatter freely.

college bed maker: a woman who acts as a servant in residential colleges (particularly at the universities of Oxford and Cambridge).

comet: a notable comet had appeared in 1769.

burning mountain: Vesuvius in Sicily erupted in 1767.

bagatelle: (French) trifle.

staring: blunt.

18 *I don't think ... look in her face:* this makes more credible his later confusion of Miss Hardcastle with the 'barmaid'.

my chief inducement down: what chiefly persuaded me to come down to the country.

prepossessing: prejudicing. Here the word is used in the sense of 'prejudicing against', whereas nowadays it is commonly used in the contrary sense of 'prejudicing in favour of'.

'prentice: apprentice.

duchesses of Drury-lane: women of low character who dressed in showy fashion and frequented the area of the Drury Lane Theatre. Prostitutes looked for trade among theatregoers.

19 *use no ceremony:* avoid formality; 'make yourself at home'.

campaign: that is, his wooing of Miss Neville.

white and gold: suits with trimmings or waistcoat of a contrasting colour were becoming particularly fashionable in the 1770s.

Liberty-hall: a house where guests may feel free to do precisely as they wish, and not be constrained by any plans or rules laid down by the host or hostess. It seems that Goldsmith invented the phrase, although the Roman playwright Plautus (250–184 BC) used a similar Latin expression two thousand years earlier.

embroidery: embroidered clothes.

Denain: a French town besieged during the War of the Spanish Succession. Nearly every detail given by Hardcastle concerning the siege is incorrect, and as it occurred in 1712 he cannot have been there himself. Goldsmith himself was well aware of the historical details (see his

History of England, Vol IV (1771), pages 166 and 178).

ventre d'or: (French) gold-fronted.

20 *cup:* wine flavoured with fruit, spices and sweet herbs.

Warm work ... elections: that is, in bribing voters with free drink.

mistakes of government: probably a reference to the difficulties of the administration of Lord North (1732–79), which was having particular trouble with India and the North American colonies.

Heyder Ally: Hyder Ali (1728–82), conqueror of large parts of India until finally defeated by the British under Sir Eyre Coote in 1781.

Ally Cawn: Mohammed Ali Kahn Walajah (1717-95), Nawab of the Carnatic; supported against the French by the British, who took over government of the Carnatic when he died.

Ally Croaker: a character in a popular Irish song.

21 *Westminster-hall:* law cases were heard there from the thirteenth century until 1882.

battle of Belgrade: a siege at which Prince Eugene (see note to page 1 above) captured Belgrade from the Turks in 1717.

22 *chuse:* choose.

how: whether you will find out what you wish to.

upon the high ropes: thinking Hardcastle to be a mere innkeeper, Hastings supposes that he is boasting in claiming one so high in rank as a colonel for an uncle.

Joiners' Company ... Corporation of Bedford: city companies and town corporations were renowned for their banquets.

supper: generally a late snack taken at the end of the day, and not a full meal. It usually consisted of cold meats.

pruin: prune.

your pig: probably not intended personally, but in the sense of any pig. This usage of 'your' occurs several times in the play.

23 *pye:* pie.

Florentine: baked dish of minced meat, eggs, currants and spices.

shaking pudding: jelly or blancmange.

taffety cream: probably a light whipped pudding, reminiscent in appearance of taffeta silk.

made dishes: elaborately prepared food.

green and yellow dinner: not clear whether this refers to the colour of the food, sauces or tableware.

assiduities: attentions, services.

24 *even among slaves:* the French were sometimes referred to as slaves before the French Revolution of 1789.

the laws of marriage: a reference to the unpopular Royal Marriage Act of 1772, which restricted relations of the king from marrying whom they pleased. William Henry, Duke of Gloucester and the King's brother, had made a private and (under the terms of the Act) illegal marriage to Lady Waldegrave, with whom he was in love. The Duke was present at the first night of the play when the audience delightedly applauded this line, taking it to be an attack on the Act.

25 *India Director:* a director of the East India Company and hence, doubtless, a very wealthy man.

Perish the baubles: I couldn't care less what happens to—such trifling toys!

teize: tease.

run the gauntlet: originally a punishment in which the offender (or victim) was made to run between a double row of men or boys who struck him with sticks or ropes as he passed along. It here refers to an ordeal of inspection or criticism from a number of people in quick succession, and retains this sense nowadays.

26 *'Offering to go':* showing a willingness to depart.

Hem! hem!: a cough or clearing of the throat as a sign of agitation.

95

27 *insure:* ensure, guarantee.

Cicero: Marcus Tullius Cicero (106–43 BC), statesman and man of letters, but most famous as an orator.

employed some part of your addresses: been engaged sometimes by you in conversation.

28 *grave and sensible:* serious and capable of sensibility (that is, emotional sensitivity).

man of sentiment: one whose breeding and fine feelings (or pretences to them) govern his conduct. In Sheridan's *The School for Scandal* (1777), Joseph Surface is a satire on the type, for although he continually pretends to fine feelings, he is in truth a thorough hypocrite.

29 *'Sola':* alone (feminine of Latin 'solus').

sentimental: refined.

engaging: persistent in pressing attentions; 'pushing'; forward.

30 *'coquetting':* behaving flirtatiously with.

'back scene': the two painted shutters which formed the background scenery at the rear of the stage.

Ranelagh, St James's, or Tower Wharf: Hastings is gently mocking Mrs Hardcastle's ignorance for, whereas Ranelagh Gardens and St James's Park were places of fashionable resort (the King lived at St James's Palace), Tower Wharf was frequented by fisherwomen and thieves.

Pantheon ... resort: a London audience would have enjoyed this display of ignorance. The Pantheon was a fashionable theatre, but the Grotto Gardens were a cheap version of the Ranelagh; and Mrs Hardcastle's admiration for the reputation of the Borough (of Southwark) shows how out-of-date she is, for the nobility had long deserted that area, which was now at best the haunt of rich tradesmen, and at worst the venue of the disreputable Southwark Fair where ladies would definitely not have been seen.

tête-à-tête: here means 'love-affair'.

the Scandalous Magazine: nickname for the *Town and Country*

Magazine, each number of which contained engraved heads of a famous man and his supposed mistress side by side, with a commentary which was full of gossip and scandal.

Miss Rickets of Crooked-lane: country ladies frequently wrote to a correspondent in London for news of latest dress fashions. Incidentally, rickets is a disease which causes crooked, malformed limbs, and Crooked-lane, in the City of London, is now renamed Arthur Street.

this head: this hairstyle.

dégagée: (French) nonchalant, informal, studiously careless.

friseur: (French) hairdresser.

Ladies' Memorandum-book: one of the contemporary fashion-books.

Such a head in a side-box: side-boxes are private compartments in the theatre which hold four or five seats. They are close to the stage, and in Goldsmith's day they rose directly from the side of the stage, and as such gave the opportunity to those who used them of fashionable display before the rest of the audience. Hastings is saying that Mrs Hardcastle's hairstyle would attract much attention – but he cleverly does not say for what reason!

Lady May'ress: wife of the Lord Mayor of London.

inoculation: vaccination against smallpox was introduced into England in about 1718 by Lady Mary Wortley Montagu (1689–1762), wife of the English ambassador to Constantinople, where she had learned about the treatment. Mrs Hardcastle's remarks indicate that smallpox scarred faces were no longer an everyday sight. Goldsmith himself had suffered from the illness when a child.

escape: that is, escape being noticed.

31 *single button:* Mr Hardcastle clings to the old style of long waistcoats, whereas the current fashion was for short waistcoats with fewer buttons.

cloaths: clothes.

throw off ... wig: wigs were going out of fashion, and gentlemen were beginning to wear their own hair.

plaister: plaster.

Gothic: barbarous, uncouth, unsophisticated.

tête: a tall, elaborate wig.

samplers: from the sixteenth century until the early twentieth century young children were taught fancy needlework and embroidery by stitching simple designs, hymns and other verses, mottoes, alphabets and suchlike with coloured wool or thread on rectangular pieces of cloth. These provided 'samples' of their skill, trained them to memorize pious thoughts, and developed (or at least tested) their patience.

Mrs Niece: 'Mrs', when applied to young girls, was a term of disapproval. However, the title was sometimes applied to elderly spinsters as a sign of respect.

fall in and out: are reconciled and quarrel again.

in another story: telling a different story, singing a different tune.

32 *before faces:* in public.

crack: there is dispute as to what this word means here. It may mean 'lie', and one editor considers that possibly it should be a stage direction indicating that Tony cracks his whip in frustration as he does not wish to call Miss Neville a liar in public. Most likely is that it means 'smart saying' (and as such is an example of eighteenth-century English usage which reappears as American slang: i.e. 'wise-crack').

cracked my head: as they stand back to back in order to compare their heights, he knocks his head against hers; and thus he repays her verbal 'crack' with one that she feels physically.

lud: Lord.–

fortin: fortune.

work: embroider with a needle.

prescribe: in the sense of giving medicine.

receipt: medicine, drug, remedy, recipe.

the compleat huswife: a popular household handbook of medicines, remedies and miscellaneous information.

coursing me through Quincy: giving me a course of Quincy's remedies. John Quincy (d. 1723) had published a home-help entitled the *Compleat English Dispensatory*, which was full of remedies and tonics.

viper: alluding to the proverbial phrase 'rearing a viper in one's bosom', used to indicate a child's ingratitude towards its parents.

dinging: dinning, repeating time after time.

33 *first day's breaking:* first day in the training of a young horse.

34 *loud as a hog* ...: she squeals as loudly as a hog stuck in a gate.

Bandbox: a showiness which comes out of her bandbox (in which her make-up would have been kept).

mun: (dialect) man.

Anon: originally this word meant 'at once' although now it has weakened into 'sometime soon' (it is synonymous with the word 'presently' in this respect). Here it has the different meaning of 'What?', 'Eh?' or 'Come again', indicating a disbelief that the hearer has indeed heard aright.

Act III

35 *piece of brass:* rude, impertinent, brazen person.

masquerade: a masked ball, where fancy dress was sometimes worn. Hardcastle probably intends an ironic comment upon the fashionable London social scene.

36 *mauvaise honte:* (French) painful shyness.

rally: are joking.

Bully Dawson: a notorious London ruffian and swindler of the time.

37 *furniture:* qualities, with perhaps an obscene quibble.

bobs: probably brooches or ear-rings with swinging pendants.

genus: possibly a corruption of 'genius' or 'Jesus'.

38 *amused:* bemused, deceived.

bear your charges: pay your expenses.

fibs: small lies, 'white lies'.

rule of thumb: a rough and ready method (such as using the thumb as a ruler).

I don't value ... cracker: I care less about her resentment than I do for the bang of a firework.

Morrice. Prance: dance off quickly. The words are derived from the Morris dance.

39 *my lady Kill-day-light, and Mrs Crump:* the lady presumably sleeps all day or revels all night, or both. A crump was a hunchback. It is ironic that Mrs Hardcastle fails to realize that these ladies take their jewels to town in order to pawn or sell them, and not on account of any fashion.

paste and marcasites: cheap imitations of real jewels.

glass: looking-glass, mirror.

rose and table-cut: two ways of cutting diamonds and other precious stones so that they will sparkle when worn; rose-cut stones have a domed surface with many facets, whereas table-cut have a flat top and bevelled edges.

court ... puppet-shew: the costly magnificence of Solomon's court is described in the Old Testament of the Bible (see Kings 7:8–12 and following). It was popularly represented as a gaudy puppet-show at Bartholomew Fair in Smithfield, London.

40 *trumpery:* worthless finery.

garnets: semi-precious stones of no great value, garnets were ruby-coloured and unfashionable at this period, considered more suitable for older women than for girls.

spark: (slang) dashing young man.

41 *Catherine wheel:* a firework which rotates and throws out bright sparks when ignited. St Catherine of Alexandria was martyred on a spiked wheel in 307 AD.

42 *Cherry in the Beaux' Stratagem:* Cherry is the innkeeper's daughter in the highly entertaining *The Beaux Stratagem* (1707) by George Farquhar (1677–1707).

but when: except when.

to market: that is, the market for a husband.

43 *cant:* language, jargon.

Did your honour call?: this and the succeeding phrases are imitations of a barmaid's language and commands.

Lion ... Angel ... Lamb: inn rooms were given names rather than numbered at this period.

curtesy: curtsy.

'tablets': writing tablets, the equivalent of a modern notebook or diary.

44 *malicious:* mischievous.

nectar: originally the drink of the gods, but used to describe any delicious drink, or the honey collected from plants by bees.

mark of mouth: a horse's age is estimated by the size and condition of its teeth.

45 *obstropalous:* obstreperous (probably, Kate is trying to affect a rustic version of the word).

dash'd: downcast.

rallied: teased.

the Ladies' Club: situated in Albemarle Street, London, to which men were admitted as guests. Clubs developed from the use of inns and coffee houses as meeting places for businessmen, literary men, politicians and other society figures. Gentlemen could quietly smoke a long churchwarden pipe, or read and discuss the contents of newspapers, which were beginning to appear for the first time. In the latter half of the eighteenth century some coffee houses developed into gambling clubs.

Rattle: chatter, gossip-monger.

'salute': that is, kiss.

Mantrap: a mantrap was a sharp-toothed gin-trap, used against poachers.

Blackleg: a slang term for a card-sharper.

Biddy Buckskin: a reference to Rachael Lloyd, one of the leading members of the Ladies' Club. 'Rachael' was altered to 'Biddy' after the first performance.

chit: pert, saucy girl.

46 *nick'd seven ... ames ace:* terms used by gambling dice-throwers: seven was a high throw; ames ace was two ones, the lowest possible throw.

hawl: haul.

Act IV

49 *above-stairs:* that is, in her bedroom.

50 *with a witness :* with a vengeance, without doubt, that's for sure.

51 *intreaty:* entreaty; that is, requesting, begging.

'*To the side scene*': Marlow speaks in the direction of the scenery to the left- or right-hand side of the stage.

sirrah: an imperative or contemptuous form of address – from 'sir'.

52 *liberty and Fleet Street:* probably alluding to the thirty-seven taverns which Fleet Street contained in the eighteenth century.

dammy: damn me.

soused: soaked, saturated, completely immersed, pickled.

banter: joke with.

A puddle in a storm: that is, much fuss about little. A modern equivalent is 'a storm in a teacup'.

53 '*bantering*': jokingly (although clearly Mr Hardcastle feels that matters have gone beyond a joke).

the Rake's Progress: a set of engravings from paintings by William Hogarth (1697–1764), depicting the progressive moral degradation and ultimate ruin of a wealthy, pleasure-loving young man.

on't: on it; that is, about it.

coxcomb: insolent, conceited fellow.

54 *caricatura:* caricature (Italian form of the word). Exaggerated cartoons of well-known people were often sold in print shops.

Dullissimo-Maccaroni: (Italian) the most stupid macaroni. A 'macaroni' was an eighteenth-century fop with affected manners and a liking for 'Continental' styles in clothes Apparently they enjoyed eating macaroni, wore red-heeled shoes, small cocked hats, close-cut jackets, waistcoats and breeches, together with a knot of artificial hair. They carried long tasselled walking-sticks. Marlow now sees himself as this kind of silly dandy – and the stupidest of the kind at that.

puppy: that is, an insufferably conceited young man.

55 *sensibly:* Marlow means that he is emotionally moved.

I stoop'd to conquer: the title of the play is supposed to have been suggested to Goldsmith by a line in *The Hind and the Panther* (1685) by the poet, essayist and playwright John Dryden (1631–1700): 'But kneels to conquer and but stoops to rise'.

56 *Whistlejacket:* a famous racehorse which won classic races at Newmarket and York in 1754.

billing: usually 'billing and cooing'; that is, kissing and murmuring like doves and pigeons, who rub their beaks together and make quiet cooing sounds.

pound: an enclosure where stray animals were placed (impounded) until their owners claimed them and paid a fine for their release.

57 *haspicolls:* harpsichord. Tony is prone to malapropisms (Mrs Malaprop in Sheridan's *The Rivals* (1775) frequently distorted long words or misapplied them).

bobbins: in lace-making, the small pegs of wood, bone or ivory (often beautifully carved) which weigh down the lace, and which a skilled lace-maker moves swiftly and skilfully to and fro in order to form the pattern of the lace.

incontinently: immediately.

mun: (dialect) must.

cramp: cramped.

58 *disguised in liquor:* written by a drunken man.

izzard: the letter 'Z'.

feeder: trainer of fighting cocks.

Shake-bag: a large fighting cock.

cut ... quite out of feather: beaten, in a cock-fighting match; stripped them of their feathers; figuratively speaking, won all the bets.

Goose-green: that is, the colour of the cock.

59 *choaks:* chokes.

nice: precise, over-clever.

60 *Bedlam:* colloquial name for a madhouse; hence, uncontrollable noise and confusion. The word is a corruption of 'Bethlehem' from the former Hospital of St Mary of Bethlehem, founded in the City of London in AD 1247, which became a lunatic asylum at the beginning of the fifteenth century.

protection ... correction: they are saying that both Tony's youth and his stupidity save him from being challenged to a duel.

baskets: single sticks with wicker-basket handguards. Perhaps the dash indicates that Marlow and Hastings are making as if to draw their swords at this point.

Act V

Scene 1

63 *will make our personal friendships hereditary:* will lead our children to inherit and continue our friendship.

65 *mortifications:* embarrassments.

66 *profest:* professed.

Scene 2

67 *smoaked:* smoked; that is, the horses have sweated so much that they have steamed.

Rabbet me: confound me, drat me. From 'rabattre' (French), meaning 'to beat down'.

varment: country dialect for 'vermin'. He is referring in uncomplimentary terms to his aunt and cousin.

mon: (dialect) man.

By jingo: a meaningless expression of surprise, used for emphasis. Originally employed by conjurors.

slough: bog, quagmire.

68 *circumbendibus:* roudabout route. A mock-Latin word, based upon 'circum', meaning 'around'.

She thinks herself forty miles off: at this point, the first-night audience of the play hissed somewhat at such an improbability; however, Sheridan, author of *The Rivals*, actually played such a trick upon a lady.

cattle: that is, horses.

whip off: get away smartly (as if by the crack of a whip).

quickset hedge: hedge of hawthorn bushes or other living growth.

69 *five that kept here:* highwaymen who frequented this place.

close: hidden.

70 *I'll lay down my life for the truth:* the motto of the French philosopher and writer Jean Jacques Rousseau (1712–78).

71 *varlet:* rogue.

Scene 3

75 *faultering:* faltering.

just to be heard: so as barely to be heard.

77 *arbitrary:* unreasonable.

gather all the poor of the parish: that is, to a feast.

Epilogue 1

78 *We have our exits…:* see Shakespeare's *As You Like It* (II. vii. 141). The rest of the Epilogue parodies Jaques's famous 'seven ages of man' speech.

hir'd: engaged by an employer at the annual country hiring fair.

I hopes as how…: an imitation of the ungrammatical speech of an uneducated country girl.

coquets: flirts with.

chop-house toast: a woman whose 'health' is drunk by men gathered in eating places.

ogling connoisseurs: men who think themselves expert in dealing with women and have the habit of eyeing them amorously.

Cits: citizens of a low, coarse kind.

gridiron: a frame of iron bars for grilling flesh or fish over a fire.

compleat: complete.

E'en Common Councilmen: even members of the Common Council of the City Corporation.

caro: literally dear (Italian), but probably used in the sense of 'bravo' or 'encore'.

79 *Nancy Dawson:* a popular song named after a famous hornpipe dancer who had performed at Sadler's Wells and Covent Garden.

Che Faro: a famous aria in the opera *Orpheus and Eurydice* (1762) by Gluck (1714–87).

Doats: dotes.

Heinel: Anne Heinel (1752–1808), a famous German ballerina who sometimes danced in London.

spadille: the name given to the ace of spades in certain card games popular at that time.

Barrister … Bayes: Mr Bayes, the main character in *The Rehearsal* (1672) by George Villiers, Duke of Buckingham (1628–87), became a stock name for a playwright. There is a pun upon 'bays', the laurel crown traditionally awarded to a great poet. Hence, Goldsmith is asking for applause for himself. There is also a rather feeble pun here upon barrister/barmaid.

Epilogue 2

80   *Cradock:* Joseph Cradock was a Leicestershire friend of Goldsmith.

nonly: only.

bobs: curtsies.

hoikes: hurries.

a'n't: ain't (slang for 'is not').

Sadler's Wells: a pleasure-garden containing a medicinal spring discovered in 1683 in the grounds of a Mr Sadler, who set up a music house there. It was replaced by a theatre in 1765. This was pulled down and in 1931 the present Sadler's Wells Theatre was built on the same site (in Rosebery Avenue) and has become famous for opera and ballet.

roratorio: his version of the musical composition known as an oratorio.

Further reading

Other works by Goldsmith

The Works (5 volumes), edited by Arthur Friedman, Clarendon Press, Oxford, 1966.
Selected Works, edited by R Garnett, Hart-Davis (Reynard Library), London, 1950.
A Goldsmith Selection, edited by A Norman Jeffares, Macmillan, London, 1963.

Criticism and biography

GINGER, JOHN, *The Notable Man*, Hamish Hamilton, London, 1977.

GWYNN, STEPHEN, *Oliver Goldsmith*, Thorton Butterworth, London, 1935.

HILLES, F W (ed.), 'Portraits by Sir Joshua Reynolds', in *The Private Papers of James Boswell*, Volume III, Yale University Press, New Haven, Connecticut, 1952.

JEFFARES, A NORMAN, *Oliver Goldsmith* (in *Writers and Their Work* series), Longman (for the British Council), London, 1959; revised edition, 1965.

LUCAS, F L, *The Search of Good Sense: Four eighteenth century characters*, Cassell, London, 1958.

Study questions

1 Find out as much as you can about the story of the first production of *She Stoops to Conquer* in March 1773.

2 Find out more about eighteenth-century sentimental comedy comparing it wherever possible with *She Stoops to Conquer*. Why do you think the popularity of the former has faded with its age, whereas the latter continues to give pleasure? (The following may be of help: the Dedication and the notes on it; the note to page 6 – *no accident ... moving*; the note to page 9 on *maxum*; the note to page 28 on *man of sentiment*.)

3 Why does Tony Lumpkin play his practical joke on Marlow and Hastings?

4 'He might have seen something in me above a common inn-keeper' (Mr Hardcastle, Act V, scene 1). Why does it take so long for Marlow to discover his mistake?

5 'In *She Stoops to Conquer* the possibilities of mistakes are explored to the full, and they follow in quick succession.' Illustrate fully the truth of this remark.

6 Analyse the way in which dramatic irony is used to give rise to much of the comedy in the play.

7 Samuel Johnson declared that he did not know of any 'comedy for many years that has answered so much the great end of comedy – making an audience merry'. Discuss the methods by which Goldsmith achieves this.

8 Hardcastle says that Tony is 'A mere composition of tricks and mischief'. Do you agree? Does Tony's character develop during the play?

9 What kind of man is Mr Hardcastle?

10 Discuss Mrs Hardcastle's character.

11 Show how some of the play's stock comic devices (for instance, the use of the screen or the reading aloud of Tony's letter) are used to show a character in a different light, or to alter a situation.

12 What is your view of young Marlow's character?

13 Compare Kate and Constance.

14 What idea does the play give us of the contrast between eighteenth-century town and country life?

A consideration of the following may help you: Mrs Hardcastle's attitude towards country people (see page 1 and notes thereon); the contrast between the 'low' country characters and the sophisticated Marlow and Hastings in the Three Pigeons scene; the notes on *grumbletonian* (page 10), *Squash-lane* and *Crack-skull Common* (page 12), *parfectly unpossible ... yeating* (page 14) and *We have laughed at that these twenty years (page 15)*, *Ranelagh* (etc.), *Pantheon ... resort, the Scandalous Magazine*, and *Miss Rickets of Crooked-lane* (and indeed most of the notes to page 30), *masquerade* (page 35), *Dullissimo-Maccaroni* (page 54).

15 Why do Mr Hardcastle and his daughter have different ideas about Marlow's character?

16 What do you think the play tells you about the arrangement of marriages in the eighteenth century?

17 What conclusions do you draw about Marlow and Hastings from their appearance in the Three Pigeons and their first meeting with Mr Hardcastle?

18 If you were producing *She Stoops to Conquer*, what scenery would you need? And what stage properties? Prove your points by referring to the text. *After* you have attempted this question it may be a good idea to find out how the play would have been staged in the eighteenth century.